KB000289

2023 CONSUMER TREND INSIGHTS

First published in the Republic of Korea in November, 2022 by Miraebook Publishing Co.

Copyright © 2022 by Rando Kim
All rights reserved. No part of this book may be reproduced, stored in a retrieval system, or transmitted in any form or by any means, electronic, mechanical, photocopying, recording, scanning or otherwise without permission of the author and publisher.

Inquiries should be addressed to
Miraebook Publishing Co.
5th Fl., Miraeui-chang Bldg., 62-1 Jandari-ro, Mapo-ku, Seoul
Tel : 82-2-325-7556 / email : ask@miraebook.co.kr

www.miraebook.co.kr
blog.naver.com/miraebookjoa
Instagram.com/miraebook
Facebook.com/miraebook

ISBN 978 89 5989 712 4 13320

2023
CONSUMER
TREND
INSIGHTS

Rando Kim · Miyoung Jeon · Jihye Choi · Hyuang Eun Lee · June Young Lee
Soojin Lee · Jung Yun Kwon · Dahye Han · Hyewon Lee · Yelin Chu · Dahyen Jeon
Translated by Hye June Yoon · Proofread by Michel Lamblin

미래의
창

Authors

Rando Kim (김난도)

Rando Kim is a professor in the Dept. of Consumer Science (DCS), Seoul National University (SNU) and the head of the Consumer Trend Center (CTC), SNU. As a specialist in consumer behavior and market trend analysis, he has written more than 20 books including *Trend Korea* series, *Trend China*, *What Consumers Want*, and *Luxury Korea* . He has also written essay books, *Amor Fati*, *Future and My Job*, and *Youth, It's Painful* which have sold three million copies in 14 countries. He has conducted research projects about consumer needs finding, new product planning, and market trend probing for Korea's major companies like Samsung, LG, SK, CJ, Hyundai Motors, Amore Pacific, Lotte, Fursys, Nongshim, and Coway.

Miyoung Jeon (전미영)

Miyoung Jeon currently works as a research fellow in the CTC, SNU. She worked as a research analyst at the Samsung Economic Research Institute. She obtained her BA, MA, and PhD degrees in Consumer Science, SNU. She wrote her PhD dissertation and subsequent articles about purchasing behavior and consumer happiness. She received 'The Best Publication Award' from the Korean Society of Consumer Studies in 2008. She is interested in tracking consumer trends in Korea and China as well as big data analysis for new product development and industrial applications.

Jihye Choi (최지혜)

Jihye Choi, PhD in Consumer Science from DCS, SNU, works as a research fellow at CTC. She has participated in many consulting projects with Korea's leading companies such as Samsung and LG, and gives public lectures on consumer trends. She currently teaches consumer behavior and qualitative research methodology at SNU. She contributes many articles and columns to major Korean newspapers and media.

Hyang Eun Lee (이향은)

Hyang Eun Lee is a Vice President of LG Electronics, H&A Customer eXperience (CX) Division, and an associate professor in the Dept. of Service Design Engineering at Sungshin Women's University. While being a corporate professional and a professor, she co-authored numerous trend insight books and is a renowned columnist for *JoongAng Newspaper*. She received a PhD in Design from the Graduate School of Arts, SNU, and a master's degree in Design Management from Central Saint Martins in London, England.

June Young Lee (이준영)

June Young Lee currently works as an associate professor in SangMyung University. He received a doctorate degree in Consumer Science, SNU. He received 'The Best Paper Award' in *The Journal of Consumer Studies*. He worked as a senior researcher in Life Soft Research lab at LG Electronics. He is a laboratory chief of Consumer Research Center in SangMyung University.

Soojin Lee (이수진)

Soojin Lee earned a doctorate degrees in Consumer Science from SNU and currently works as a research fellow at CTC. Prior to joining the center, she was a stock market reporter on *Maeil Economic TV*. As a contributing researcher, she is conducting a number of consulting projects with Korea's major companies such as Samsung, LG, etc., and received 'The Best Publication Award' from the Korean Academic Society of Financial Planning in 2018. Also, as a lecturer she teaches consumer culture and consumer psychology at SNU.

Jung Yoon Kwon (권정윤)

Jung Yoon Kwon currently works as a research fellow in the CTC, SNU. She obtained her BA, MA, and PhD degrees in Consumer Science, SNU. She academically explored the intergenerational transmission of consumption styles in her PhD dissertation. Her interests include rapidly changing modern society, its impact on consumer cultures, and various research methodologies to capture them.

Dahye Han (한다혜)

Dahye Han is a PhD candidate in Consumer Science, SNU and is currently a senior researcher at CTC. She received a BA in Psychology, SNU and an MA degree in Consumer Science, SNU. With her master's thesis, "A Study on Consumer Emotion Changes in Online Clothing Purchasing Process," her research interests focus on consumer behavior, trend analysis, and consumption psychology.

Hyewon Lee (이혜원)

Hyewon Lee, a PhD candidate in Consumer Science, SNU and is currently a senior researcher at CTC. She worked at Dasan Books, Leadersbook, and Kakao Page Corp. for over 15 years. She has an MA degree with her thesis: "Comparative Analysis of Age Effect, Period Effect and Cohort Effect - Focusing on Consumer Perception Toward CSR." She is currently interested in generation theory and changes in consumer behavior due to technological advances.

Yelin Chu (추예린)

Yelin Chu received an MA degree in Consumer Science, SNU. Currently, she is attending a PhD program and serves as a senior researcher at CTC. Her master's thesis was about "A Study of Consumer Experience on the Online Education Service with Conditional Tuition Refund." She is interested in analyzing big data to distill insights from unstructured data, and in deriving further meaning from participant interviews through qualitative research.

Dahyen Jeon (전다현)

Dahyen Jeon is currently working on her PhD and is a senior researcher at CTC. She received a BA degree in Fashion Industry at Ewha Womans University and an MA degree in Consumer Science at SNU. She was awarded first place in the Korean Society of Clothing and Textiles (KSCT) contest in 2019. Her area of interest is consumer behavior in digital retail environment. Her current research focuses on online visual cues and haptic imagery.

Consumer Trend Center, Seoul National University

Consumer Trend Center (CTC) was established in 2004 to analyze rapidly changing consumer trends and has announced "ten trend keywords" every year since 2007. CTC has done collaborative research with numerous business firms and also offers educational programs on analyzing consumer needs. CTC plans to be incorporated with the consulting firm, "The Trend Korea Company," which specializes in trend forecasting, generation studies, marketing, and new product/service development.

RABBIT JUMP
A crouching rabbit jumps higher – take a leap!

Challenges surround us. The pandemic, which has been shaking up our lives over the past three years, is still ongoing and the economy is deteriorating. It is a repetition of the economic cycle which follows the stages of recovery → growth → slowdown → stagnation. The question now is where exactly in this cycle our economy has arrived at and how quickly it can recover. An analysis of several leading economic indicators, such as stock prices, due diligence index, long- and short-term interest rate differences, and PMI (purchasing mangers' index) reveals that the global economy is showing signs of entering a complete slowdown or recession according to NH Investment & Securities research fellow Baek Chan-gyu. This is especially the case in the United States. As inflation soars, interest rate hikes continue. The US Consumer Price Index (CPI) is at its highest level in

30 years since the 1980s, and the 10-year US Treasury yield is also at an all-time high of 3.5%. Consumption is also shrinking. While real household income declines, e-commerce sales decline as well and outstanding credit card payments rise. Indicators across the board are negative regardless of which side – macro/micro or production/consumption – you look at. The National Bureau of Economic Research predicts that the US economy will hit the bottom of a recession in the first half of 2023.

Considering that the Korean economy tends to lag the US economy by 1 or 2 quarters due to its high dependence on exports, one can infer that the Korean economy will continue to slow in the first half of 2023 and then bottom out in the 3rd or 4th quarter. Thus, the economy is unlikely to show significant improvement throughout 2023. There are warnings of an economic crisis. The economic forecasting model developed by the *Maeil Business Newspaper* and the Korea Economic Research Institute using six leading economic indicators, such as trade balance, exports, producer price, cyclical change in leading economic indices, KOSPI index, and BSI (business survey index) estimated the probability of an economic crisis comparable to the 1997 Asian financial crisis occurring within the next year to be 66% as of July 2022.

The geopolitical outlook is just as dark. The war in Ukraine looks to last longer than expected, through to

2023. From an economic point of view, the focus of this war is not "when will it end" or "who will win" but "how long will sanctions on Russia last?" If strict economic sanctions against Russia continue and Russia keeps gas exports to Europe cut off, it will have an ongoing economic impact on Europe and in turn the global economy. Geopolitical tensions between China, Taiwan, and the United States are also intensifying. While it is unlikely that China will invade Taiwan as some worry, there remains the probability of small provocations and localized conflicts continuing between the three countries. It is likely that 2023 will be a complicated year for South Korea, which faces a difficult dilemma due to its high political and economic dependence on the US and China.

Describing the international political and economic order of the 30 years following the 1980s is something akin to describing a "flattening earth." Through the WTO and FTA agreements, trade barriers between countries were lowered and political conflicts eased. However, those times in which the economy came first are coming to an end. Now is the time when the political reasoning of each country takes a front seat ahead of market efficiency, says Shin Hwan-jong, managing director of Korea Investment & Securities. The pandemic has especially accelerated this trend. Countries are building up barriers between themselves and ideology is increasingly becoming more important than pragmatism.

During such times, making interpretations or forecasts based on just "quantitative economic analysis" as in the past becomes difficult. The complete picture can only be seen when including an analysis of "geopolitical risk." It complicates any type of prediction, and that is while 2023 is approaching with an overwhelmingly negative outlook.

What patterns will repeat and what will change

The year 2023 reminds me of 2008 in multiple ways. 2008, the year of the global financial crisis that was sparked by the US subprime mortgage crisis ended up destabilizing the world. Stagflation, a combination of inflation and recession, threatened the global economy. As global oil prices soared, consumer prices rose rapidly. In Korea, the won once hit around 1,500 won per dollar, and the trade balance also deteriorated rapidly. There was the Russo-Georgian War, and a global drought that led to a food crisis as agricultural product prices soared. 2008 was also the year of government change in Korea from the Roh Moo-hyun administration to the Lee Myung-bak administration. As the number of unsold homes increased and the property market went into decline, the new conservative government loosened the previous government's strict housing market regulations to increase the housing supply, cut property and transaction taxes, and relaxed reconstruction regulations and fees.

There are also many differences between the two periods.

Today, the fundamental health of the Korean economy has become much stronger, and industries that are competitive on a global level such as semiconductors and batteries have been established, as have sectors that are serving as new growth engines in the K-content field of entertainment and games. Now, as we attempt to forecast the consumer trends for 2023, it is crucial to distinguish between what will be repeated from 2008 and what will change.

Recession consumption typically follows a set pattern. First, consumer spending decreases and demand for lower-priced goods increases. The main keyword in 2008 was "reasonable," as people looked for reasonable prices and values. It was also in 2008 that the Spanish fast fashion brand Zara, which offered fashionable products at a reasonable price, entered Korea. Uniqlo, which had entered the market earlier, also began to show explosive growth in sales at this time. It is notable that the discount offers for fried chicken at large supermarkets became popular again from the middle of 2022. Additionally, consumption habits that emphasize practicality, such as packing a lunch box, the "zero-spending" challenge, half-off discounts, and choosing home-cooked meals over dining out or ordering delivery, are on the rise recently.

The two keywords that describe fashion trends during recessions are "retro" and "instinct." During an economic boom, experimental and bold styles or fashion emphasizing silhouettes are mostly popular, but during recessions, retro styles or styles that emphasize physical attractiveness gain popularity. Currently, retro "Y2K fashion" and nostalgic products like "Pokémon Bread" are trends among young age groups. Until recently, miniskirts had been the typical items that came into fashion during recessions, but this time around we are witnessing an "underboob" trend. The trend has just shifted from bottoms to tops, and still follows the formula of recession fashion trends that focus on emphasizing physical attractiveness. In the publishing sector, finance and investment books, or self-help and counseling-related content that comforts readers tend to be on the bestseller lists during a recession, and in other sectors, instinctive and stimulating items tend to grow in popularity. In addition to counseling-related books, cosmetics featuring bright colors, contraceptives, and sweet-flavored alcohol and liquor with high alcohol content are gaining popularity. In conclusion, several recent consumer trends are already mirroring those typical of recessions.

However, a recession does not necessarily translate to a decline in overall consumption. Instead, the luxury market tends to grow and not just because income disparities are widening. This is because demand for so-called "small luxury" items, products that create new demand, remain strong even during recessions. Therefore, even amid a recession, new growth opportunities can be found if the market is viewed through a detailed breakdown by consumer segment, rather than from a broader perspective. 2023 is said to be a year of recession, but there have been significant changes over the past few years. There have been rapid technological advances, and new apps, virtual worlds, remote work, and the digital economy have all developed significantly. Moreover, a generational change is taking place with the main consumer group now moving towards Generation MZ. Thus, the key is to anticipate what kind of new trends will arise when these ongoing changes collide with the cyclical economic downturn.

Times when typical consumption patterns disappear

We have derived the top 10 consumption trends for 2023. The ten trends can be divided along three axes: economy, people, and technology. (1) Changes arising from the shift in direction of Korean society and market changes due to the recession (Disappearing Average, Cherry-sumers, New Demand strategy); (2) changes in values due to the emergence of a new generation (Office Big Bang, Index Relationships, Digging Momentum, Generation Alpha, Neverland Syndrome); and (3) changes in retail distribution and space (Proactive Technology, Real Space) are the topics we explore to see how they influence trends of 2023.

The most striking change in our society in recent years is the disappearance of what used to be called "typical." We have understood groups on the premise of a so-called "normal distribution" in the basic shape of a bell, with the largest number of points surrounding the "mean" in the center and decreasing frequency as it moves away from the center. So, if companies were to come up with something that matches this average value well, they would be able to secure the largest number of customers. However, this concept of normal distribution is breaking down. Polarization, which is frequently discussed these days, is a representative example. During a recession, people look for heavily discounted products, but at the same time the ultra-high-end luxury market tends to grow along with it. It is just the "average" mass market that is shrinking. In the era of people rejecting these typical products, it is difficult for companies to survive by continuing to cater to what they consider an average audience. Exceptional measures are required. The first of the keywords of each year's edition encompasses the broader trend of the year, thus the "Disappearing Average" trend was introduced as the first keyword for this year.

Next, we look at the general characteristics of consumption during recessions. As in the aforementioned example of the growing demand for discounted fried chicken in large supermarkets, consumers in a recession have been known to seek cost-effective purchases, but in 2023 this phenomenon is expected to be taken to the next level. By actively utilizing apps and platforms, consumers no longer focus solely on the price factor but strive to get what they want at the lowest cost. Consumers who diligently collect the benefits of corporate marketing offers and memberships without making actual purchases are called "cherry pickers." Along these lines, today's consumers who pursue cost-effective consumption by joining up with other buyers and splitting the products and costs will be called "Cherry-sumers." The term "cherry picker" has some negative nuances of being overly opportunistic. But the "Cherry-sumer" is a more neutral evolution of a cherry picker and focuses on the new type of consumer looking for cost-effective choices.

Should companies focus solely on offering low-cost products in order to get consumers to spend? This is not the case: in a recession, consumption choices are made in a selective and focused manner. Essential purchases for daily use are made in an extremely cost-effective manner, but for products that people desire, consumers do not hold back. How do companies reach consumers' hearts and minds in that regard? Amid a recession, it is difficult to raise prices too much in an attempt to make a product part of the premium segment. So, a new strategy is needed to create new demand. The "New Demand" strategy is an effective methodology for companies to go about product improvement that will create consumer demand to both replace old products and buy exciting new products.

As pointed out earlier, although there are many similarities between the recessions of today and 2008, the biggest difference between then and now is the change in the driving force of consumption. The biggest cause of change in the market, both among households and in the workplace, is the emergence of a new generation, commonly referred to as Generation MZ. During times when people say even a three-month gap is enough to cause what feels like a generational gap, it is a tough task to aggregate the 30 years' worth of generations from 1980 to 2009 under one label, Generation MZ. But it is this new generation that is driving major change in every element of our society.

The place where that change is most obvious is in the workplace. In the United States, the number of resignations is increasing rapidly to the point of being called "The Great Resignation," and the organizational culture in Korea is also changing significantly. We call this trend the "Office Big Bang" in the sense that changes surrounding work and organizational culture are happening at an exponential rate. The Office Big Bang phenomenon not only discusses the recent increase in job turnover, but also explores the root cause of the growing number of resignations. We then highlight fundamental and practical ways for companies to attract and retain talent.

One of the most important aspects of human life as a social being is establishing relationships. In the past, we have classified relationships on a straightforward scale by distinguishing between close friends and acquaintances depending on the closeness of the relationship. However, as various types of social media are being used simultaneously, the distinction between these relationships is not as simple as in the past. Moreover, due to the impact of the pandemic, in-person encounters have significantly decreased, and as a result the layers and depth of personal relationships have become very complex and multidimensional. The new form that relationships take can be referred to as an "Index Relationship" in the sense that relationships do not just have the differentiating criteria of "being close" or "not being close" but are managed by attaching an index label to the relationship based on that relationship's purpose. This new aspect of establishing and managing relationships will have a profound impact not only on personal relationships but also on trends across our economy, including consumer behavior and work life.

Humans have a natural tendency to be preoccupied with a subject. Whether it's work, love, or a hobby, we find meaning in our lives when we are fully absorbed in something. This is a universal phenomenon that transcends time, but there is something special about the level of preoccupation of the younger generations. As the recently popular word "over-immersion" suggests, it is about finding, discovering, expressing, and showing off oneself by being fully immersed in a certain topic. This phenomenon is called "Digging Momentum." The word "digging" goes to describe not just the activity of mining into a subject but also of discovering one's own raison d'être in the process of digging deep.

This youthful mindset is not exclusive to the younger generations. It is something we are seeing among their forebears, including Generation X and the Baby Boomers. A desire to stay young is becoming the greatest virtue and aim these days. In the story of Peter Pan, Neverland is where Peter Pan and his friends, who never grew old and remained children, lived. Korea is now experiencing "Neverland Syndrome" where everyone wants to stay young. This is not just a matter of getting plastic surgery and focusing on appearances. Young thinking is being accepted and respected across the board. We will see that there are both positive and negative aspects of Neverland Syndrome.

The youngest generation in our society is Generation Alpha. Since they are the generation after the last letter of the alphabet, "Z," it was back to the beginning for Alpha (α). Those born after 2010 also deserve to be called Alphas because it signifies the beginning of a new human tribe as they are the first truly digital and mobile natives among us. Since Generation Alpha is still young, parenting and education of this generation are important duties. Their millennial parents are showing a new trend in parenting. The eldest among Generation Alpha are elementary school students, and we will take a look into the lives of this new generation through the keyword "Generation Alpha."

Going back to the parallels with 2008, the most important reason for there being many different aspects between these two periods is that technology has developed significantly since then. Technological development has reached levels which were unthinkable 15 years ago and has gone beyond just making daily life convenient – technology is indispensable for survival. For example, without digital platforms, how would the economy have continued to function during the pandemic over the past three years? This series has selected and taken in-depth dives into notable technologies every year. Until now, technology has developed in the form of offering a solution to daily needs. Now, by analyzing highly personalized big data with artificial intelligence, it is evolving in the direction of preemptively identifying and responding to needs before they occur. We call this "Proactive Technology."

The evolution of virtual space along with technological advancement is astonishing. Virtual space is not just a medium of communication, it is becoming a new ground for human life, including commerce and political expression. How should the concept of "space" be redefined? What will the future of real-world space be, that is often discounted as something that is merely offline? How will new virtual spaces, including the metaverse, develop? The power of "Real Spaces" contains the answers to these questions. During an era of virtual worlds, Real Spaces actually prove to be stronger. What is the essence of that power?

Year of the Black Rabbit: prepare to jump forward

2023 is the Year of the Black Rabbit. Rabbits are small and shy herbivores, so they give people the impression of being timid and weak. But in many anecdotes, they are characterized as being strategic and smart. There is also a local saying that expresses the rabbit's wisdom: "a cunning rabbit digs a hole with three caves." It means they have a plan B and a plan C lined up in times of crisis. In today's words, it can be translated as being good at hedging risk and not putting all your eggs in one basket. In preparation for the economic and geopolitical challenges expected in 2023, it is good to use the wisdom of the cunning rabbit.

Rabbits don't walk. They jump. They have big ears and bright eyes, so they can hear and see well. While examining alternatives to describe the overall trend of 2023 with 10 characters, I particularly liked the image of "jumping." Although we are facing a difficult new year, we decided on "RABBIT JUMP" as the title of the book and main keyword, with the hope that we jump and act wisely like a rabbit. It contains hope that the crouching rabbit will be able to jump higher, although it may be hampered by the recession. If we endure this period well, there will be a chance to take another leap forward.

In elections, loyal votes are often referred to as "domesticated rabbits," and floating or swing votes as "wild hares." The same will be true in the market. If loyal customers are called domesticated rabbits and new customers are called wild hares, in today's chaotic market, where consumer brand loyalty is weakening every day, even holding on to domesticated rabbits has become a difficult task. Furthermore, it is an increasingly difficult task to catch wild hares, which has changed significantly from the past. How do companies attract consumers when they cannot predict their next move? This has become the challenge for all.

The color of this year's cover is yellow. In folk stories, it is said that rabbits live on the moon. The color of the moon, which has symbolic ties to the rabbit, was thus chosen. People make a wish when they see the moon. Rather than gradual improvement, destructive and disruptive innovative thinking is often expressed as "moonshot thinking." As a color that can convey these themes linked to the moon, I thought that yellow was the best color. I hope that 2023 will be the year when all our readers' wishes come true.

"The greatest danger in times of turbulence is not the turbulence; it's to act with yesterday's logic."

Following the words of Peter Drucker, the most dangerous thing during these times is to believe past success is the equation for future success. Scholars call this thinking "hubris" and warn of extreme caution. Lee Byung-nam, former CEO of consulting group BCG Korea, said in his book *Common Sense* that "in most industries, 'trend extrapolation' is typically used to predict the growth potential of the next three to five years. It is a way of predicting industry growth trends using those of the past by assuming they will continue for years to come, but unfortunately the reality is often the opposite." Now, as industrial conditions enter a new phase every two to three years with new competitors emerging due to the volatility of the industrial cycle, "systems and practices must be overhauled every three years."

Ships are safest when they are docked. But that is not the reason ships exist. Although 2023 is expected to be a year filled with heavy storms, perhaps that crisis can be an opportunity to look back at our roots. In the Year of the Rabbit, whether we can make a leap or not depends only on whether we can innovate. The crisis itself is not the problem. Our attitude towards it is. In the era of transformation, the relative word of "change" is not "remain." Now, the options we have are either "change or die."

Rando Kim
Professor, Department of Consumer Science
Seoul National University

CONTENTS

Redistribution of the

The average is losing significance. To elaborate, the mean, which is typically used as a representative measure of a group, is becoming meaningless. This phenomenon in which the average loses its position as a standard can be seen in three different situations: (1) "polarization," where values are concentrated at two extremes; (2) "multipolarity," where individual values are widely scattered; and (3) "unipolarity," where values all lean toward one side.

The driving force behind the Disappearing Average trend is structural. Capitalism inherently causes a divide between the rich and the poor, but as the pandemic has contributed a differential effect for more than two years, polarization has accelerated in nearly all areas, including the economy, society, education, and culture. The emergence of the platform economy has further boosted polarization. The platform economy is highly dependent on economies of scale and investment in digital technologies. That makes barriers to entry even higher, and as a result the winners at the end of the competition are scarce. The "winner-take-all" phenomenon has intensified.

What was previously considered normal products, ordinary lives, mainstream opinions, and societal norms are all changing. The mass market, also symbolized by a normal distribution, is now on life support and is evolving into a market that requires irreplaceable excellence, significant differentiation, and diversity. The strategy companies should take will be one of three options. First is taking a clear side in the direction towards one of the two extremes; second is customizing strategies to provide optimized utility to a small group (sometimes just one individual); and third is building a wide ecosystem or network that competitors cannot imitate – a winner-take-all strategy. It is time to "redistribute the average" and recognize its non-normal, varied, and diverse components that reflect the tastes of an increasingly individualized society.

The average is losing significance. It has become difficult to use words such as "normally," "generally," "usually," or "on average" about a phenomenon happening around you. This is because lifestyles are greatly diversifying. In online communities, there are frequent posts from people asking how much money is appropriate for their acquaintance's wedding gift, or how many dates they should go on before asking to go steady or confessing their feelings. Such questions about even the most basic of life's problems highlight the disappearance of what was previously considered the "average" answer that everyone takes for granted.

This trend is not just evident in personal life. The standard of good products, mainstream opinions, and what constitutes as "normal," which until now has been expressed as an average value, is on shaky ground. People instead gravitate toward extremely unique products and are split by strong opinions on both ends of the spectrum. As the distinction between what is normal and abnormal is starting to become accepted as being "different" rather than "wrong," and as the world starts to view and value diversity more positively, the idea of something being normal and average is gradually losing its place. In *Consumer Trend Insights 2023,* we will call the phenomenon of the disappearance of the "normal" standard that has been widely accepted in the market and society, as well as in the lives and values of individuals, as the "Disappearing Average" trend.

Average measures of everything from grades to age, education level, wealth, income, life expectancy, average return, weight, IQ, etc., have been common concepts until now. This is because mass production and mass consumption became common after the Industrial Revolution, and with the emergence of a standardized education system it became the accepted way to classify individuals in a single homogeneous group. However, at a time when the scientific management of workflows aimed at improving efficiency (historically known as "Taylorism") is shaken to the core by artificial intelligence and big data's overhaul of many industries, there is a pressing need to revisit the concept of the average.

"Nano Society," the first keyword of *Consumer Trend Insights 2022,* shed light on the characteristics and trends of individuals and lifestyles that were scattered in small units. The keyword "Disappearing Average" of this book seeks to capture the new redistribution of this scatter. Other trends that are introduced in this book, such as the seismic shift in the workplace ("Office Big Bang"), innovation that overturns market dynamics ("New Demand strategy"), relationships that are reclassified based on tastes and lifestyles ("Index Relationships"), complete immersion in narrow interests ("Digging Momentum") are all new trends that have their foundations in the emergence of a whole new type of distribution. To talk about the phenomenon of the Disappearing Average, let's first take a look at what the "average" actually means.

When the Definition of 'Average' Changes

The mean is one of the representative values used to make sense of data, and it is mainly used to summarize a dataset in which many individual values are gathered into a single number. For example, when comparing the incomes of Korean and Japanese people, it is difficult to look at all the individual incomes separately; but if you find the average, comparisons using a single number are possible. In fact, the mean is a concept frequently used in daily life. However, in order to use the concept of the mean, we must presuppose a normal distribution.

"Normal distribution" refers to a distribution in which the data forms a bell-shaped symmetrical distribution with the mean value at the center. An important characteristic of normal distribution is that the center bulges in the y-direction so that most of the data values are concentrated near the center. Statistics says that 68.2% of all values fall within ±1 standard deviation from the mean and 95% within ±2 standard deviations. Simply put, the mean is the most common, and the further away from the mean, the less common the value. Therefore, in a normal distribution, the mean represents what is quantitatively the majority and qualitatively typical, serving as a standard to show the members of the distribution where they are currently located and where they should be headed.

But what if this basic premise of a normal distribution is broken? As shown in the figure below, the mean is not suitable for representing the data that is non-normally distributed. The first chart shows a polarized bimodal distribution, in which the median value corresponding to the mean represents the smallest number. The second chart is a distribution that has multipolarity where individual values do not have a specific pattern of correlation and are scattered. The third figure is a distribution called unipolarity, in which there is a single value that is significantly larger than the rest and a majority of values that does not have any other meaningful correlation to the large values.

In all three cases, the mean does not serve as a representative value for the population, defeating the purpose of the mean. Let's look at some examples of polarization, multipolarity, and unipolarity, and why the mean has lost its traditional meaning.

polarization	multipolarity	unipolarity
average	average	average

Polarization:
The Disappearance of the Midpoint

The fate of capitalism: polarization

A widening wealth gap is an inescapable feature of capitalism. Capitalism, which is based on the premise that "homo economicus" serves their self-interest, has helped develop the economy we know today by seeking efficiency. This has also resulted in the inevitable polarization of wealth. In addition to these intrinsic attributes, the development of the network economy and the pandemic, which will be described in detail later, have further exacerbated polarization.

Polarization can be seen in asset values. When breaking down property tax figures collected by Seoul districts in July 2022, the property tax in Gangnam-gu was shown to be the highest at 413.5 billion won and 17.5 times higher than the property tax levied in Gangbuk-gu, which had the lowest at 23.6 billion won, showing the largest gap on record. Property taxes in the three districts of the Gangnam area, including Gangnam-gu, Seocho-gu, and Songpa-gu, account for 39.0% of the total property tax in the 25 districts of Seoul. Asset polarization among the young age groups is even more serious. According to data released by Statistics Korea in 2021, the average wealth of the bottom 20% of household heads in their 20s fell by 11.9% compared to 2020, while the mean wealth of the top 20% increased by 2.5%. The wealth of the top 20% in their 20s and 30s is about 35 times that of the bottom 20%. The gap is seen to have been exacerbated by wealthy Generation MZ inheriting real estate from their parents, while there were others in the same age group that faced losses from their failed investment strategies.

Just as consumers' wealth is divided, the market is equally divided. While consumer demand for products at ultra-high or ultra-low price points has increased, the number of consumers looking for mid-range products is decreasing. In the US, department store group Macy's and the US version of Daiso, the Dollar Tree, enjoyed a significant increase in operating profit in the first quarter of 2022, up 178% and 43%, respectively, compared to the previous year. Meanwhile, Walmart recorded an 18.2% decrease. Amid the competition between the ultra-high end and ultra-low end, mid-range products have lost ground. This polarization trend is also reflected in the performance of domestic department stores and hypermarkets. Department stores, which mainly sell luxury goods, recorded a 16.8% year-on increase in sales in the first quarter of 2022, while hypermarkets had a year-on decrease of 1.9%, making it the only segment within the retail sector to show negative growth. Meanwhile, it is notable that the sales of self-branded products, which are at low-end price points among the three major supermarkets' products, increased by 8.5-10%.

When the economy is contracting as it is now, consumers tend to reduce unnecessary spending and focus their resources at the extremes. With the return of the "*jjan-tech*짠테크" craze, which is a recession-type consumption trend, people use and buy exactly as much as they need. The number of mobile gift certificates with a value of less than 5,000 won on second-hand trading platforms increased sharply, and the sales of prepared meals at large supermarkets between January and July 2022 increased by 25% compared to the same period the previous year due to people trying to cut down on the cost of eating out. Meanwhile, the premium market is also growing rapidly, led by the younger generations. They are spending money that they have saved in other areas for special experiences. Frozen desserts at hotel lounges costing around 100,000 won, Korean beef omakase priced at over 200,000 won, and luxury hotel suites priced at 1 million won per night are all enjoying a boom, expanding on the "small luxury" trend.

A similar phenomenon can be seen in investment strategies. For example, the "Barbell strategy" stands out in the financial market. This refers to an investment portfolio with both extremely safe assets and extremely risky assets, as if lifting a barbell with weights concentrated on both ends. It is a strategy that pursues both profitability and stability during uncertain economic times where the risk of recession and inflation coexist. Equity traders have been known to make big windfalls by ignoring the mean. Here, traders choose the strategy to focus solely on the trends of individual stocks while ignoring the benchmark stock index, which represents the average measure of the market. European investor André Kostolany explained his investment philosophy by saying that an averaged index chart of the broader market is like a doctor's crazy idea of analyzing a chart of the average body temperatures of all his patients combined instead of individual charts for each patient's temperature.

A similar trend can be seen in cinemas. Experts have analyzed and shown that while ticket prices at theaters have risen due to the pandemic, more people are accustomed to enjoying movies on streaming services. Movies are now being divided into cinema movies, where the full audiovisual immersive experience from large screens and sound systems are worth the expensive ticket price, and streaming movies, which are good enough to enjoy at home.

The length of the content is also being polarized into

short form and long form. As short-form content, which can be consumed quickly and easily in videos clips of less than a minute, has become a trend, the average monthly usage time of TikTok users in the first quarter of 2022 experienced a year-on increase of 40%, exceeding that of YouTube. As a result, both YouTube and Instagram are increasing their focus in the short-form video formats known as "Shorts" and "Reels," respectively. That is not to say, however, that the number of people who enjoy long-form content and prefer in-depth content has decreased. In recent years, the running time of a movie has typically been two hours, and in some cases three hours. Also notable is that blogs, which are a representative example of long-form content, are making a comeback. In 2021, Naver Blog will have 2 million new blogs and 300 million related pieces of content. This is an increase of more than 50% compared to 2020.

Increasing political and social polarization

The phenomenon of divergence into two extremes is not confined to economics and finance. Of increasing concern is polarization in the political and social sectors. At the 2022 Kyunghyang Forum, best-selling author and historian Jared Diamond said that political polarization is the biggest challenge facing today's society. In the United States, the polarization of political ideology has been on the rise for a long time, and some see it as even affecting the mortality rate. Because each state and each county can be backed by different political parties and policies, the mortality rate in Republican-backed counties was found to have decreased by only 11% compared to Democratic-backed counties' decrease of 22% from 2001 to 2019. Each state has different health policies that affect health depending on the party they support. For example, differences in whether or not Medicaid applies, the minimum wage, tobacco and gun control, and drug addiction-related health policies can be shown to have an impact on health and mortality. It is sometimes expressed as "party polarization" because support for a certain party becomes so strong that these ties rarely change. It is problematic because party support stems from negative partisanship in which hatred of the opposition party is a far stronger motivator than any positive emotions for the supported party.

Korean society is not free from political polarization either. According to the Korea Institute of Public Administration, while ideological polarization among people supporting opposing parties did not deepen, it was reported that the emotional polarization between the supporters of the two main parties had increased since the mid-1990s. In particular, among twenty-somethings the concern is the clear divide in ideological inclination according to gender, which may spark social conflict. This can be linked to parties and politicians somewhat preferring to maintain an antagonistic symbiotic relationship that incites conflict, which in turn helps them gather votes. Under the "winner-take-all" single-choice election system, in which the candidate who gets even one more vote is elected, this situation is not without benefits for political parties. In addition, social media plays

〈 Political and social polarization of twenty-somethings in Korea 〉

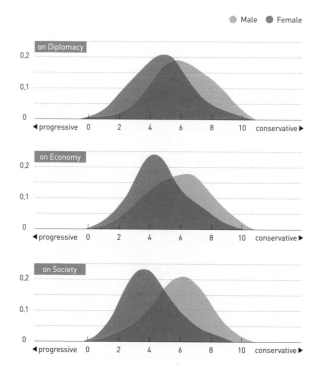

Source: JoongAng Ilbo, 2022.01.25.

a role in intensifying political and social polarization due to the echo chamber effect that results from people listening solely to news and opinions that match with their opinions.

Polarization aggravated by the pandemic

What we have long regarded as an average day has changed dramatically since the pandemic. The pandemic has accelerated polarization in multiple sectors that have been described so far. The pandemic changes the pace, not the direction of the trend.

City streets, which had been quiet due to social distancing, have gradually started returning to their former bustling liveliness after the second half of 2022, but there is a difference in degree of the rebound depending on the commercial sector one looks at. Spaces that focus on activities are crowded with people who have been craving entertaining experiences, but functional spaces that were used for events such as dinner parties and study groups are not as lively as before, as virtual platforms have taken over this role. Many organizations have also begun to reinterpret the workplace. For example, short-term homestay platform Airbnb classifies employees based on the functions of their roles, and all employees (except those classified as essential workers) have been relegated to remote work arrangements. Regular in-person events and functions are held to encourage socializing and build rapport between members of the organization.

The place where the polarization of non-face-to-face daily life is most noticeable is the educational sector. First, as more students become distracted during online learning classes, the number of mid-ranked students that have fallen below the level of basic academic ability in performance evaluations has increased. Middle school students in particular demonstrated a typical polarization pattern in which the middle performers disappeared while the higher and lower performers grew simultaneously. The polarization of academic achievement is closely related to the polarization of the private education sector.

According to the results of the 2021 household trend survey by Statistics Korea, spending on education including private tutoring and academies is one of the items that recorded the largest year-on growth at 14.1%, and spending on private education stands out among them. Students with the highest grades (within the top 10%) spent 485,000 won per month on private education, while those with the lowest grades (the lower 81-100% of students) spent 270,000 won. In addition, while the cost of private education increased in large cities, it fell in small- and medium-sized cities. More than 80% of high-income households making more than 8 million won a month spent money on private education, but less than 40% of households that made below 2 million won a month spent money on private education. Many parents said that they send students to private academies not only to bridge the learning gap that came from the shift to online courses but also to make friends because, unlike in schools, these academies continued to operate face-to-face classes which allowed students to meet and interact with friends. This suggests that the effects of polarization in the educational sector is not a straightforward issue.

Multipolarity: Diverse Scatter

"Obscurify: How obscure (or basic) is your Spotify?"

The time when the Top 100 charts on music sites were everyone's favorite songs is long gone. Global music streaming platforms like Spotify go beyond providing a list of the most popular songs and utilize algorithms to recommend music based on your music tastes. A Spotify-linked application called "Obscurify" goes a step further, analyzing the user's music taste based on their Spotify usage history and compares it with other users to give them an "Obscurity rating" that shows how unusual and unique the user's music taste is. If people in the past just followed the public's tastes by looking at the Top 100 charts, it's clear now that they prefer their own niche music reflecting their unique tastes, far from the normal distribution of popular songs. And in terms of distribution, diverging musical taste can be said to display "multipolarity," in which data points are spread diversely across multiple frequencies.

Many consumers, many tastes

The trend of multipolarity can be found not just in music streaming but wherever personal taste is important. A typical example is the shift in the restaurant industry. As the quality of dining-out options has improved, ranking restaurants based on how tasty their food is has become less meaningful. Now, the search for a restaurant has turned into the search for a "cool restaurant," so the competition is fierce among restaurants to offer different concepts and styles. They compete to find their unique wedge in the market, whether it be a local restaurant with a long history that offers a classic taste, one that provides fresh visuals and interior design, or one that promotes a healthy lifestyle with high-quality ingredients and sophisticated recipes. Consumers looking for a more unique experience are looking for hip places only a select few know about, not "hot" places that are just crowded with people.

Publishing, where the term "bestseller" originated, is also moving towards multipolarity based on individual tastes. A publishing industry expert now says that when planning a book, the target becomes about 2,000-3,000 readers whose sales are guaranteed rather than hundreds of thousands of mass-market readers. This is partly due to the increasing challenges the publishing market faces, but it is also due to the demand for books having become highly segmented. Reflecting this trend is the recent popularity of pocket-sized paperbacks in Korea. Although they are small and light, the book's theme is specific enough to attract the curiosity of readers and cater to niche tastes. A typical example is the "*Anyway*아무튼" series, which deals with only one narrow subject, such as Mangwon neighborhood in Seoul, grand-mothers, or socks. They also have a subseries called "*Thing*명," which deals with just one everyday topic, such as black bean noodles, Pyongyang cold noodles, or cheese.

The growing number of neighborhood bookstores also exemplifies multipolarity. Although offline bookstores are facing challenges due to competition from online book-stores, small independent bookstores are on the rise. The number of registered independent bookstores has continued to grow from 97 in 2015 to 745 in 2021. Independent bookstores with unique personalities play a role beyond simple distribution and sales, providing recommendations for different tastes and a unique forum for sharing and communication. On the subject related to Spain, for ex-ample, there are various bookstores, such as the "Spanish Bookstore" in Chungmu-ro, Seoul, which handles a wide range of books ranging from travel guides to textbooks for Spanish exams. Or there's the "Reading Center" in Mangwon neighborhood, which rents out their space, holds book club meetings, and even lends books out for free. There's a bookstore for everybody.

There are changes being made to apartment floor plans which have always been a prime example of where uniformity and the average, normal standards had long been applied. A floor plan of an 84 m^2 apartment normally featured two rooms, a living room, a bathroom, and a kitchen. Now it is possible for consumers to install makeshift walls or open existing walls according to their personal tastes. It is also possible to change the interior structure, including the bathroom and kitchen, even after having moved in. The era of bespoke options for apartment floor plans is now here. The average number of different floor plans of 186 apartment complexes sold nationwide in the first half of 2022 reached 5.73. Among them, 22 apartment complexes (11.83%) offered 10 or more different layouts, which is up from the 7.55% of apartments that did so in 2019. Construction companies that emphasized floor-plan diversification outperformed in terms of sales performance and the average subscription ratio of 90 complexes that offered 10 or more layout types was oversubscribed 36.11 to 1. This reflects survey results that show "internal floor plan layout" is the most important factor considered when choosing a home.

Diversification of lifestyles

As the Korean societal view of marriage and the family changes, lifestyles are also diversifying. The reason it is difficult to refer to Generation MZ as a single group with singular characteristic is that several groups with distinctly different lifestyles are included within the same generation. Some dream of owning a house early in their 20s and value financial preparedness, while others feel fed up in their careers and make their hobbies the focus of their lives, satisfied with short-term happiness. Others move abroad to expand their professional scope. The "right answer society," in which most people used to pursue one model answer, is being divided into multiple worlds where people seek their own unique answers.

Accordingly, differentiated corporate benefits, such as how detailed a company is when it comes to taking care of the diverse lifestyles of its employees, has become an important factor when selecting a job. Previously, employee benefits mainly focused on offering summer vacation resorts for families of four, parents' health checkups, and financial support for children's education. But now, companies are increasingly making sure single households don't feel left out. In addition, customized benefits such as housekeeping services and pet insurance are provided. The location of work and the type of work are also becoming important elements of lifestyle choices. For office workers who experienced the advantages of remote work during the pandemic, commuting to and from work five days a week is no longer seen as the default form of work, but rather a factor that requires a considered choice.

An important point the multipolarity phenomenon brings to the surface is that what is considered typical and standard in society is disappearing. Korean society, which has historically had a strong conformist nature, has shifted towards a culture that values the individual, and as such the path of life, which used to have a "must-follow" sequence, is becoming more open to individual choices. As a result, the reference group that people seek to emulate is also diversifying. Here, social media plays a significant role in helping users find an archetype that suits them while at the same time serving as a venue for them to display their own lifestyles and tastes. Under this backdrop, the average measure of the group becomes less significant, simply becoming one option out of many.

Unipolarity: Moving Toward One

Question: What do the following number sequences show?
① 0% → 92.49%
② $150 million → $469.8 billion

The answer for ① is Google's early (1998) to recent (2021) market share of internet searches in the US; and ② is Amazon's early (1997) to recent (2021) total sales. In 1998, when Google was founded, it was a latecomer to the scene, with Yahoo already accounting for about 50% of the search engine market. But now, Google is a monopoly with more than 90% of the market. Amazon started out as an online bookstore in 1994, and in 1997 it turned into a small online retailer by expanding its scope to include CDs, clothes, furniture, and toys. However, in May 2020, it accounted for 38% of all U.S. retail e-commerce transactions, surpassing that of Walmart, which ranked a far second at 5.8%.

A third type of breakdown of normal distribution occurs in the case of unipolarity, which pulls everything into one pole like a black hole. The distribution created by such unipolarity is also called a "power-law distribution." The characteristic of a power-law distribution is that there is no limit to the values of outliers in the dominant position. People do not consider global tech giants such as Google and Amazon to be one of the many companies that turned out to be a fad, growing rapidly and just disappearing one day. Marketing professor Scott Galloway, an early prognosticator for the global trend of unipolarity, pointed out that tech giants' exceptional dominance became more extreme as they experienced a boost from the pandemic, calling the process "collective selection." The strong became stronger and the weak disappeared from the market. Five of the major global tech giants (Microsoft, Amazon, Apple, Facebook, and Google) account for 21% of the market capitalization of the US stock market.

All paths lead to the platform

The area where the phenomenon of unipolarity is most commonly found is the platform economy. As of 2022, KakaoTalk, which started its service in 2010 in Korea, is the most frequently used app by Koreans (99.6 billion messages a month) and is unrivaled among its competitors in the app market. The same is true for video platforms. In 2008, P2P (peer-to-peer) platforms were sharing the market with Pandora at 42%, Daum TVpot at 34%, and AfreecaTV at 23%. Now, YouTube has monopolized the market, becoming the most-used app by duration use for Koreans (74 billion minutes per month). For the winner of these tech wars, it is not enough to simply say that the platform services that have dominated the market are the top companies. The fact that verbs such as "to google" and "to Ka-talk (the shortened version in Korean for 'KakaoTalk')" have emerged, as well as the profession of "YouTuber," means that these platforms have become inextricably linked to people's lives.

Now, the phenomenon of unipolarity is showing signs that it can occur not only in platforms but also in traditional industries. Among the self-employed and sole proprietorship market, the winner-take-all phenomenon is getting stronger, which is also largely influenced by the digital shift. Although digital transformation has the effect of lowering barriers to entry for smaller companies and expanding sales opportunities, it also creates a so-called "superstar" effect in which demand is concentrated only on a few exceptional products as the scope of competition online expands.

Unipolarity in the platform economy is an unavoidable trend for both platform providers and participants. Metcalfe's law is a theory that explains how one company can become more powerful as the network grows. The value of a communications network is proportional to the square of the number of its users. The value of the network increases exponentially, not linearly. Economies of scale are changing qualitatively, in which the cost of production per unit decreases as the scale of production increases. The Barabási-Albert model shows that all networks grow by a process of "preferential attachment," where the more connected a node (or "hub") is, the more new links it will likely receive. When explained in terms of a participating seller on a platform, it means that the seller is more likely to want to sell at a global fair where there are more opportunities to showcase their products than at a local neighborhood market. Consumers also prefer places that offer more options and are attracted to products that more people have chosen. That's because the fact that something has been chosen many times acts as a strong signal to attract more buyers. Following Alberto-Laszlo Barabási's Third Law from his book *The Formula*: "past success × fitness = future success."

As the world becomes increasingly connected, the phenomenon of unipolarity sometimes appears in the form of a mania. As information spreads instantly, the strength and speed of a fad or trend becomes stronger and spreads faster. When considering the release of a movie in the past, there was a time difference in release dates between countries, so the box office performance in other countries played an important role in garnering attention for the film. Now, movies are released simultaneously through video streaming platforms and the global content rankings are updated in real time and announced daily. Content that tops these global rankings acts as a powerful magnet that makes people want to watch it too.

Outlook and Implications

"100 soldiers reached a river they were about to cross. The general commanding the soldiers received reports that the mean height of the soldiers was 180 cm and the mean depth of the river was 150 cm. He decided that they could march across and ordered them to cross the river. But in the middle of the river, the water suddenly became deeper, and the soldiers began to

drown. The general, who realized the situation too late, ordered a retreat, but had already lost many soldiers. It turned out that the deepest depth of the river was two meters."

This story shows just how fatal errors can be when solely relying on averages. To avoid falling into the trap of averages, one needs to look at various statistics that further describe the data to get the full story. As with the river-crossing story, the maximum value (maximum depth) and minimum value (the height of the shortest soldier) may have proved to be the most important numbers needed to make the right decision and save lives. As such, the most appropriate data necessary – perhaps the median, mode, or standard deviation – may differ depending on the situation. Before analyzing data, it is essential to understand the nature of the situation and the data. No matter how advanced the statistical techniques are, an accurate answer cannot be found without understanding whether the data meets the conditions for a normal distribution or a skewed distribution.

Until now the average has served as a commonly used standard and criterion. People often compare their income with the average of their group, as if they were assessing the level of their success. The average figure is oddly reassuring. When a person is above the mean, they feel relieved, and when they are below the mean, they become anxious. Although this comparison can sometimes play a positive role for self-reflection and motivation, it is now necessary to examine whether such comparisons are still appropriate. Todd Rose, president of Boston-based think tank Populace, stresses the point that the days of focusing on averages and evaluating people as a point on a normal distribution is over, and that we need to adapt to the age of individuality.

Average-based thinking tends to lead to one of three errors. First, people can fall into a "one-dimensional mindset" that evaluates people based on just one average statistic. Characteristics of people are independent of one another. For example, a person's height and hand size are not proportional. Therefore, it is necessary to understand several aspects or metrics on a three-dimensional scale. Second, it is possible to overgeneralize and make assumptions from categorizing or grading individuals based on a normal distribution. This can be compared to trying to explain all of a certain person's behavior by solely using MBTI, even though everyone behaves differently depending on the context. For example, gauging a woman's preferences and behavior when visiting a restaurant may be more closely related to whether she's with her family or alone, rather than the classification that she is an office worker in her twenties. Third, people may get caught up in "normative thinking," or conforming to norms, by living according to what the average standard is. The average measure only provides a snapshot of a certain point in time, not the whole process of how to live.

For companies and institutions that need to identify specific targets, the trend of the Disappearing Average will make it difficult for them to find a safe and conservative strategy. Until now, most companies have prioritized targeting the mass market. As the word "mass" suggests, the target has been a large, amorphous collection of individuals, and the target in the mass market was an unspecified "anyone and everyone." Now, when normal distributions are no longer what they used to be, it is highly probable that the mass is just an illusion. In times of polarization, multipolarity, and unipolarity, "average," "typical," and "normal" are just ambiguous terms. The strategy companies need to take now will be one of three: choosing a clear side among two extremes, customizing strategies to provide optimized utility to a small group (sometimes that will be just one individual), and finally, building a wide ecosystem or network that competitors cannot imitate in a winner-take-all strategy.

Companies cannot stand out with average ideas, typical products, or normal services. Normal products, lives, opinions, and standards that can be expressed as averages are actually changing. As the mass market, which was based on a normal distribution, is shaken to the core, markets need to offer irreplaceable products, differentiation, and diversity. If things remain average, companies will fail. It is time for a new strategy to be sought by identifying and strengthening each of a company's core competencies and targets and to get them in line with the changing landscape of the industry from the ground up. It is time to "redistribute the average" and recognize its non-normal, varied, and diverse components that reflect the tastes of an increasingly individualized society. It is only when companies are armed with something extraordinary, far outside the ordinary, that they can achieve success in a market stagnated by recession.

Arrival of a New Office Culture:
'Office Big Bang'

The workplace is undergoing revolutionary change. Talent is leaving, and organizational culture and labor market systems are changing. Because these changes surrounding work are happening at an explosive rate, we will call this trend the "Office Big Bang."

Among the shifts taking place as part of the Office Big Bang, the most notable phenomenon is the retirement craze. 62% of new hires are retiring after less than three years at a company. "The Great Resignation" is a global economic trend that affects Korea as well, where switching jobs has now become an effective way to manage careers, according to a 2021 survey. Efforts by organizations to retain talent amid rising turnovers and resignations are a hot topic. Higher salaries and bonuses are the basic minimum, and tailored corporate benefits that match the lifestyles of young employees are being made a priority. More fundamentally, the ability to structure an organizational culture and create a work environment conducive to retaining young talent will be key. Furthermore, the number of workers that do not belong to an organization is increasing. The growing number of freelancers and gig and platform workers due to rapid digitalization of industries.

The Office Big Bang can be attributed to two factors: the declining value of salaried work due to the rapid rise in asset prices, and the adaptation to new ways of working during the pandemic. Another important point to note is that with the entry of a new generation into the labor force, the previous generations' identification with their organizations no longer applies. What used to be "the growth of the company is equal to my growth" has shifted to a more individualistic value of "my personal growth is more important than the growth of the organization." The Office Big Bang will spark a chain reaction of changes not only in the workplace, but also among individuals, organizations, and markets in the future.

If the CEO of a company said the following, what would your reaction be?

"Everyone at Tesla is required to spend a minimum of 40 hours in the office per week. Moreover, the office must be where your actual colleagues are located, not some remote pseudo office. If you don't show up, we will assume you have resigned."

The remarks are part of an email Tesla CEO Elon Musk sent to his employees in May 2022. It effectively ends work from home. And it's not just Tesla. As the U.S. and Europe ease quarantine and social distancing measures, major companies are moving in the direction of preferring employees to be back in the office. Starting with US credit card company American Express in March 2022, large US companies including Google and Apple are requesting employees to return to the office. The UK government officially ended work-from-home guidelines in January 2022. So, how are employees responding to the CEO's request?

"I quit."

Attitudes toward quitting are changing too. Recently on YouTube, videos from employees in their 30s and 40s quitting their jobs are gaining popularity. On Instagram, the hashtag #resignation is on the rise. The number of voluntary resignations in the U.S. stood at a record 4.54 million in March and 4.4 million in April, according to the U.S. Department of Labor. A similar trend can be seen in an episode of a current affairs program, titled *Generation MZ, Leaving the Company* which aired on KBS in July 2022. In the episode, when asked about what benefits the company offers, a CEO emphasizes that it offers student financial aid for children of employees. Regarding this, one employee says:

"I don't even plan on getting married, but a student loan... Do you expect me to work for 15 or 20 years?"

The labor market is changing. Topics such as remote work, hybrid work, and flexible commuting are frequently discussed among the office worker community. Employees are starting to think more about personal preferences around how they work, and not just about the salary. More people are changing jobs in search of their preferred working conditions, and companies are facing challenges in recruiting and retaining talent. Companies are desperately trying to recruit talent and prevent turnover among their top employees. However, the number of gig workers who refuse to join organizations full time despite companies' efforts for change is rapidly increasing. Workers wanting to generate additional income outside their main jobs or to leave the labor market early are some of the changes breaking the stereotypes of a traditional career's duration and form. In *Consumer Trend Insights 2023*, we call this trend the "Office Big Bang" in the sense that changes at personal, organizational, and system levels in the workplace are happening at an exponentially expanding rate.

Professor Anthony Klotz of the Graduate School of Business at Texas A&M University, who predicted the mass exodus of workers after the pandemic, says that the pandemic has become an opportunity to reconsider the definition of work. The pandemic only accelerated the shift to remote work, but it also sparked fundamental questions about work-related topics that had long been unquestioned. The pandemic was the decisive moment that brought the Office Big Bang to the forefront of people's minds, and it revealed the underlying demand and desire for change in the way people work. The Office Big Bang in 2023 is becoming a trend that has people questioning themselves about what work is, and at the same time gives them the chance to contemplate what the roles of individuals and organizations should ideally be amid this time of rapid change in organizational culture.

A Series of Explosions in the Office

The Office Big Bang occurs as a chain reaction. In the beginning, it may appear like a small number of individual changes, but the impacts of these changes have a knock-on effect on the organization that causes catastrophic changes in the system. The change led by a few individuals have sparked the "Great Resignation" that is now set to lead to an overhaul of the entire organizational culture. All this has the potential to transform the labor system as a whole. Let's take a look at each of these stages of the chain reaction.

The individual: Liberation notes from the office

Employees are quitting. Although it has been a long time since the concept of working at one company in a lifelong career has disappeared, the number of years employees stay with a company has been declining in recent years. The average length of employment at large companies was 8.2 years at the end of 2003, according to online employment portal Job Korea's analysis of the top 103 companies that year. Meanwhile, 75.5% of respondents were found to have experienced job turnovers, and three out of ten people left without completing a year of joining the company, according to a "first job change experience" survey of 343 male and female office workers in their 20s and 30s in 2021.

*"Nakalacubaedangto"*네카라쿠배당토

This mysterious sounding word is derived from combining the first syllables of the Korean names of the companies Naver네이버, Kakao카카오, Line라인, Coupang쿠팡, Baedal Minjok배달의민족, Daangn Market당근마켓, and Toss토스: the companies that Generation MZ most want to work for these days. Recently, the definition has changed to also mean that people want to work at all these companies in that order, after which they quit and start their own business.

This quitting phenomenon is not just a problem at the individual level. The Korean workplace culture is changing to have a more positive view in regards to turnover and quitting. In the past, people had been concerned that frequent job changes would contribute to them being perceived as someone who couldn't fit into an organization. Now the concern has shifted to being seen as an incompetent person if they are *unable* to change jobs. Quitting has become a part of the career development process in which people can actively explore and find the work conditions that they want most. A big data analysis of keywords like "job change이직" and "quitting퇴사" found in the news, Twitter, and online blogs and other communities between 2019 and 2020 by Konan Technology supports this trend. Compared to three years ago, the number of mentions of "job change" and/or "quitting" has nearly doubled, and the positive perceptions of the terms have increased. This change of perception is also supported by the statistics. When employees who have worked for less than three years at a company voluntarily change jobs, their hourly wage increases more than that of workers who have not changed jobs, according to labor market data from the Korea Employment Information Service. This proves that young workers are able to increase their salary by switching jobs.

Voluntary resignations are also increasing among civil servants in the public sector and state-owned corporations, which were once regarded as enviable jobs. In particular, it is notable that the ratio of workers quitting among twenty- and thirty-somethings is increasing. 5,961 people aged between 18 and 35 submitted their resignations in 2020, which is a significant increase from 4,375 in 2017, according to the Government Employees Pension Service. The proportion of people that quit with less than five years of employment also increased from 15% in 2017 to 21% in 2020.

Getting into public sector jobs is tough. So why would they voluntarily give up their dream jobs which they worked so hard for? Experts blame the conservative and rigid organizational culture of public sector organizations. Members of public service organizations reported stronger dissatisfaction than employees of large corporations in all fields, according to the "Survey on Organizational Culture" by public opinion survey company Next Research. When asked if they had ever received work requests through social media, phone calls, or text messages outside of business hours, 26.7% of employees at private companies answered that they have had such an experience, compared to 42.9% of employees in the public sector. When asked "Is there a manager that you cannot communicate with?", four out of ten civil servants (41.3%) answered "yes."

With quitters on the rise, the job search platform market is booming. Remote coaching services catering to employees planning their exit from the workplace are also on the rise. Business card management app Remember is operating a career recruitment and job search service called "Remember Career," and job platform companies such as Job Planet also provide a recruiting service that offers job change proposals if users upload their résumés. The IT industry is actively operating an internal referral system that compensates employees who have recommended talent. The retention rate of new employees is higher if they are recommended by employees who are familiar with the internal workings of the organization, according to a human resources manager in the IT industry.

People who don't plan to stay in the company for a long time don't like promotions. At Hyundai Motor Group there is even an internal term, *"jingeoja*진거자*,"* that is used to refer to employees that refuse promotion to become managers. The reason for these employees avoiding promotions is that when an employee becomes a manager, their salaries are converted to a fixed annual salary system that could be subject to restructuring at any time due to reviews based on a five-step personnel evaluation system. In addition, many employees prefer to remain as union members and receive guaranteed employment until their retirement age. This phenomenon reflects the changing values of the younger generations who put their personal preferences and lifestyles first compared to the older generations whose priority was getting recognized by the company's management.

2. Organization: Benefits over salary

Changes among individual workers also lead – in a chain reaction – to changes in organizational and human resources management. As the number of employees who are quitting (and who at least want to quit) increases, companies are looking for ways to retain them. According to a survey of job seekers by career platform Saramin사람인 in February 2022, the most important criteria for choosing to work at a company were high salary (25.7%), corporate benefits (19.6%), and company growth potential (17.8%). Salary was the number one consideration. Therefore, many companies have started to offer salary increases or high-performance pay. Many companies have been betting on cash to retain employees, such as dramatically increasing salaries for junior-level employees, with bonuses reaching as much as

1000% of the base salary.

The problem is that such increases in salaries or bonuses raise controversy over equality and fairness in the organization. Moreover, money on its own is not the strongest selling point. So, what else do they need to offer? The answer is personalized benefits. Kwon Ki-wook, a professor of business administration at Konkuk University, says, "salary is no longer the sole attraction for Generation MZ." He continues, "it is a given to be paid for the amount that you work, so in addition to salary, employees are very interested in the benefits offered by the company, especially those that make them feel that the company is taking good care of its employees." The above Saramin survey results also revealed that the younger the employee, the more important benefits become as the criterion for choosing a job.

As a result, companies are busy creating their own sets of benefits that differentiate them. The key is to introduce highly customized benefits that reflect the lifestyle of employees in their 20s and 30s. NCSoft offers student loans for young employees who have just graduated from college, and game development company Pearl Abyss provides housekeeping and pet insurance for employees living alone. The Seoul office of the Simmons Bedding Company operates a "Half Day" system where employees work only four hours every Friday morning so that they can have the rest of the day off for self-development and hobbies.

Much effort has been put into renovating the office space to attract employees who have become accustomed to working from home after the pandemic. In the United States, a trend called "resimercial" is spreading. "Resimercial" is a new term that combines the words "residential" and "commercial" and refers to decorating office space as if it were a home. It is part of an effort to replicate the convenient work environment people enjoyed at home during the work from home days.

The problem is that despite efforts by companies to offer conducive work environments, many employees still want a hybrid approach that gives them the flexibility to choose between working from home and working in the office. According to a survey conducted by Naver on post-pandemic work of 4,795 employees at its headquarters, the number of employees who wished to work in a hybrid approach was 52.2%, which was more than those who wanted to work from home five days a week (41.7%). Only 2.1% preferred to go to the office five days a week. As a result, Naver decided to try a hybrid work plan, in which employees choose their own work week, splitting between working from home and going to the office three times a week. In the United States, the hybrid work trend is spreading from big tech companies. Google had wanted employees to be in the office three times a week, but the system has been changed so that employees can work remotely for up to four weeks, and Apple is also planning to have employees come into the office three times a week while allowing work from home. Twitter encourages people to go to the office but gives employees the option to work remotely if they wish. Microsoft, which reopened its offices in March 2022, allows teams to make the decision on how to split time between telecommuting and coming to the office.

3. The labor market: The great freelance era

More people are choosing to be freelancers and to loosen ties with organizations. They are not looking to change jobs in the hopes of securing better conditions. They don't want to be part of any company. Freelancers have always existed in some industries, but since the pandemic more people are voluntarily choosing to be gig and platform workers, or so-called "nomad workers." It is the era of the freelancer.

Gig labor is not just limited to some occupations such as delivery and courier services but is now expanding to specialized areas such as marketing, development, and design. In Korea, Wanted Gigs, Wishket, Talentbank, Kmong, and Soomgo are the main platforms providing related services. A total of 250,000 experts in 11 fields including design, IT/programming, video/photo/editing, and marketing are signed up to Kmong, a platform that connects expert talent with those that need them. In the third quarter of 2021, transactions on Kmong increased by 47% compared to the same period the previous year.

The best part about gig work is the freedom to work as much as one wants, whenever one wants. There is no nagging boss, and no wasted energy trying to push for changes at the organizational level. The shift to platform labor is a reflection of the growing need for a break from organizational stress.

The number of so-called super freelancers receiving high pay is also increasing. A "super freelancer" is a concept coined by the Software Policy & Research Institute in December 2021 and is defined as a person who has a strong reputation in their respective industry and receives high compensation by working on a project-by-project basis. It is a concept related to the general freelancer who receives sporadic projects and earns an irregular and low wage. When we think of super freelancers, we usually think of IT developers, but recently they have been active in various fields such as business development, management strategy, and marketing. They are also in high demand in the fields of accounting and legal services. According to industry insiders, this group's annual income exceeded 100 million won as of July 2022, which is a 20% increase over the previous year.

Companies increasingly prefer to "lease" talent rather than hire them. Core tasks such as advanced IT development are also increasingly being outsourced. This is because projects can be started and completed quickly without having to go through a time-consuming and complicated internal recruitment process to form a new team. According to a BCG Henderson Institute survey of 673 senior executives and executive-level managers between 2019 and 2020, more than 90% of respondents rated the use of digital freelance platforms as "very important" or "somewhat important." More than 50% of the respondents answered that the utilization of the digital talent platforms would increase significantly in the future.

Background

Paradigm change due to the pandemic

The pandemic is an important turning point behind the emergence of the Office Big Bang trend. The increased risk of virus transmission in crowded spaces became an opportunity to test out remote work. Although the pandemic has become endemic, employees that have adapted to the new work styles during the pandemic are starting to question the return to the office, where efficiency could take a hit. The question then becomes whether the work setup before the pandemic was indeed the best option.

Asset prices such as real estate, stocks, cryptocurrency, and art, which have soared during the pandemic, are also considered to be factors that have accelerated the Office

Big Bang trend. Due to surging asset prices, office workers who have made significant returns on their investments no longer feel the need to work. People in their 20s and 30s are interested in the success stories of the so-called "investment gurus" who hit the jackpot. On YouTube, stories of self-made fortunes by ordinary office workers are everywhere, and books covering the investment craze are popular in bookstores. This is the result of the younger generations who are realizing that they may not be able to live on just their salary without also investing in assets such as stocks and property, actively looking for ways to secure additional sources of income.

Soaring asset prices also play a part in demotivating people who have missed out on the investment boom. The rapid rise in asset prices has even sparked a movement to reject labor completely in parts of the United States and Europe. The value of labor has been on a relative decline compared with asset prices, and young workers who have had the chance to experience the work-life balance during the pandemic are starting an "anti-work" movement in which they either give up or refuse to work. They rely on income from social services, such as state subsidies, or pay living expenses through gig work. The number of these types of quitters further increases turnover.

A new generation enters the labor market

"I want to know why I got an A⁺."

A student came to my lab to check their grades. Until now there have been occasional requests by students to know why they got a C, but this was the first time a student visited and was genuinely curious about why they received an A⁺. A new generation of students born after 2000 are curious about the "process" of how and why they received the score that they did, as much as getting the certain grade. They are a generation that values feedback.

A generation seeking procedural fairness is entering the labor market. Shin Jae-yong, a professor of business administration at Seoul National University who has studied performance evaluation and compensation, defines the "fairness" that Generation MZ wants as "the fair exchange of inputs and outputs." Since Generation MZ has grown up amid fierce competition from when they were young, they place high importance on a system's fairness to properly evaluate and communicate the value of their time and effort. Therefore, for this generation of workers, performance pay is not a gift bestowed on them by the company, but a fair reward for their efforts. In addition, it is crucial for them to understand why the bonuses were paid, with justifications needed to understand payments to each position and department. They require feedback on how each person's input was evaluated in order to understand and accept the compensation system.

Changes in people's priorities are also an important factor in causing the Office Big Bang. The shift is putting more importance on personal growth than organizational growth. Generation MZ, after witnessing two financial crises, has learned that companies do not guarantee the future of individuals in times of crisis. The reason why people consider quitting or changing jobs is not due to a lack of enthusiasm but is because they consider it beneficial and useful to spend that time at a company that will help them build better skills. That makes it important to figure out which companies are the ones that will help people grow and increase their competitiveness in the market.

Then there are young office workers who value self-reliance in managing their careers. One of the driving factors behind the Office Big Bang is that many people have started working on "side projects" or are preparing to start a business. A side project can be software development, book publishing, or education in a new subject as part of self-development outside the job. Self-branding is another popular activity. Until now, self-branding was done through social media, but recently, more options are growing. Employee career platform Remember has launched a service called "Insight" that curates business columns within online communities. As of September 2022, about 350 office workers are working as influencers and writing columns about their job change experiences, business insights, and industry trends.

Outlook and Implications

Controversy over "quiet quitting" is increasing in many parts of the world. "Quiet quitting" can be summarized thusly: "I do my job, but I only do what the job requires and no additional tasks. Although I do not actually resign, I no longer care about my evaluation or competition within the company." Both the cause and reception of quiet quitting are a mixed bag. Some criticize it as "irresponsible behavior of underperformers," while others take it as "rejecting the popular belief that work is the center of life." On the other hand, *Harvard Business Review* views it as less about an employee's willingness to work harder and more about a manager's ability to build a relationship with their employees.

The Office Big Bang phenomenon highlights the fact that the changing paradigm of organizational management must come from the bottom up. The answer does not lie just in figuring out how to retain talent. Korean organizations face the tall order of preparing for a completely different organizational culture from what they have been used to.

Creating a new organizational philosophy

The most important task is to enable members of an organization to grow on their own. Toss, one of the most popular companies among jobseekers, is famous for its intense workload according to employee reviews posted on anonymous office community and forum platform Blind. Toss does not deny the claims. "If you value job stability and comfort over all else, it will be difficult for you to feel happy at Toss," read a post on the company's promotional social media account. Nevertheless, the reason why the company is popular is because it provides ample opportunities for self-development compared to other companies by giving them responsibility for their work and guaranteeing autonomy.

Second, companies must work to gain the trust of the members in the organization. Retaining employees is not simply a matter of offering a high salary. Talented people can easily leave the second they get a higher offer elsewhere. Now, the role of HR specialists in organizations becomes increasingly important. Their role has expanded beyond hiring and managing employees to also encompass the role of an in-house communicator who delivers organizational values to employees. HR experts emphasize that just as the role of the chief financial officer (CFO) grew in importance following the 2008 financial crisis, the opportunity for the chief human resources officer (CHRO) to join the ranks of C-suite executives has arrived.

Third, communication is essential for building trust. As mentioned earlier, during times where the need for procedural fairness within the organization is becoming a necessity, any guideline now needs to be a result of ample communication, not a unilateral decision. Recently, companies have been emphasizing the need for sufficient communication between management and employees. For example, Woowa Brothers우아한 형제들 operates "Wooa Han Talk," a quarterly interactive discussion session between the company and employees. When the company needs to make a decision, the session is used as an opportunity for the company to listen to the opinions of employees and to offer background details about the decisions. Lotte Shopping has also been holding tea meetings two to three times a month called "Let's Enjoy Spring Water" since March 2022. The key is moving away from one-way communication towards open communication that can contribute to the improvement and development of the organization.

Finally, this change in organizational culture must be linked to the reorganization of KPI, or Key Performance Indicators. This quantitative indicator that tracks the progress of a team or organization against important business goals is characterized as being specific and measurable. The problem is that as the business environment and consumption trends change rapidly, the responsibilities of company divisions become blurred and collaboration between teams becomes necessary, making it difficult to measure performance quantitatively. There are times employees lose sight of the broader direction as they rush to meet KPIs. As an alternative to this, many companies are introducing "OKR," an acronym for "Objective Key Result," which is a goal-setting framework that supports tracking of results in the context of broad organizational goals. Even if it is not necessarily OKR, the method of measuring employee performance can drive and determine the direction of the organization, so it is crucial to rethink performance measurement metrics that are appropriate for the Office Big Bang era.

Remaining tasks

Changes in work patterns affect people's lifestyles. In *Rush Hour,* a book that deals with commuting from a cultural anthropological perspective, author Ian Gately writes that during a cholera epidemic in London between 1854 and 1866, many workers left the city with their families in search of a cleaner living environment. It is theorized that it is here where the modern meaning of commuting to work in the city was born, as people started commuting on the train from their houses in the suburbs 30 to 40 kilometers from the city. The concept of time in the modern sense was also formed then. For example, in the Middle Ages people usually enjoyed dinner around 3 or 4 in the afternoon after having had a big breakfast. The concept of lunch is said to have been born when people started commuting to work. Also, chapters of novels were divided around this time into suitable lengths to be read during the daily commute.

Just as cholera gave birth to the work commute, the pandemic is also changing the basics of work. As the concept of time changed and affected multiple industries as people commuted by train, the Office Big Bang is also redefining the meaning of work and sparking change. A chain reaction that affects not only workers and companies, but also consumer lifestyles and related industries should be expected. Organizations, policy makers, and society as a whole have a long list of tasks to complete to prepare for these revolutionary changes.

First, institutional support is needed. As of 2022, remote work is not fully legalized in Korea. This is because the Labor Standards Act assumes that the place of work is done in a physical workplace. In Europe, as discussions on remote work started from 2000, they have made progress in terms of making preparations including amending relevant laws. For example, in France regulations stipulate that companies must negotiate with remote workers to establish a time frame during which they can be contacted; and Portugal prohibits employers from contacting employees by phone, text message, or email outside of working hours, except in some exceptional circumstances. In addition, as the labor market becomes more flexible, it becomes an urgent task to overhaul the current system for gig workers. Measures such as preparing standardized contracts with clear terms and conditions will need to be followed to ensure their labor is valued fairly.

Most of the changes discussed in the Office Big Bang thus far have mainly covered office workers. Telecommuting or hybrid work is a change that can only be applied to some industries or jobs. It is a fair point to say industries that are unable to freely move their working spaces are frequently marginalized during discussions of new ways of working. A few IT companies, start-ups, and conglomerates are behind many of these frequently discussed trends, and it should not be interpreted as if they represent the entire labor market.

Finally, we should think deeply about how the Office Big Bang affects individuals. As working arrangements and the labor market change rapidly, each of us must think and decide where, when, and how to work more efficiently. In the midst of a whirlwind of change, surviving the shift is important, but it is just as important to find a way to take action to turn a crisis into an opportunity.

The Office Big Bang is both a process and an opportunity for people to figure out what work values are most important for each person. Most people have to work for a living. Actively exploring what makes each of us tick and figuring out what is most enjoyable, rather than being mindlessly stuck in a job, will be the best strategy to overcome the looming changes and crises.

Born Picky,

Cherry-sumers

During a time in which the global economy is undergoing a contraction, consumers are focused on making purchases that are cost effective. Consumers who only selectively take advantage of benefits without making actual purchases are sometimes called "cherry pickers." A new economic consumer trend that has been spreading amid the current recession has emerged in which consumers pick and choose their purchases in a way that makes maximal use of their limited resources. We call this group "Cherry-sumers." The consumption habits of these consumers are different from those seen in past recessions.

Cherry-sumers like to take advantage of a "divvying strategy." Small packaging and sample kits, for example, are popular because they provide an alternative from existing consumption methods, allowing people to buy just the amount they need. Next, a "half-and-half strategy" in which people join together to make bulk purchases promotes savings. Using platforms to make group purchases is one popular method to this end, as is finding people who will split fees such as delivery costs. Finally, Cherry-sumers look for flexible contracts through a "flexi-strategy." This includes choosing subscription services that can be started and canceled at any time, buying products with flexible refund policies, and utilizing savings accounts with ultra-short-term deposits.

The emergence of the Cherry-sumer is directly related to the worsening economic situation. However, it is also a structural change that favors smaller portions and more flexible consumption as the number of single-person households grows. This suggests that it is not a temporary change caused by the economic downturn but a trend that will persist. Moreover, Generation MZ is playing their part in accelerating the Cherry-sumer trend. If Cherry-sumers were once seen as just a small segment of consumers looking for shortcuts in a recession, it is now time to change that perspective.

"If I don't watch a video streaming service, I cancel it immediately. If there is something I want to see, then I start it again."

Video streaming services, such as Netflix, TVing, and Wavve, are now equivalent to traditional TV, so it is only natural that people keep their subscriptions running continuously. However, recently more and more users are choosing to stick to a periodic subscription plan that only resumes when they are actively watching the shows. And it's not just with streaming services: long-term contracts are becoming a burden. So, ultra-short-term contracts are preferred, and flexible contracts with no penalty – even if reservations are canceled just a day prior – are even more preferred. With the goal of sticking to a "no waste" life, consumers are trying to pick out the core of what they really need and to purchase just that.

Unprecedented inflation and falling asset values have pushed the global economy into a recession. As a result, consumer sentiment has deteriorated rapidly, with markets flashing warning signs. The emergence of frugal consumption is perhaps natural given these times. There is so much to buy but resources are limited, and more consumers are hoarding cash to weather tough times. Rather than following traditional consumption habits, consumers are looking for new ways to spend while simultaneously maximizing utility. The pursuit of extreme cost-effectiveness is establishing itself as a separate consumption trend that is set to influence several industries.

People who do not make actual purchases and only take advantage of peripheral benefits a brand has to offer are sometimes called "cherry pickers." It is a metaphor for taking only what is beneficial, just like picking out only the sweetest cherries on a cake. From the point of view of the consumer, this can be seen as a form of smart consumption; but from the point of view of the company, the habits may not be very conducive to sales. Cherry picking, which focuses solely on the maximum value that consumers can get, was considered problematic as some people consumed in a "take it and run" manner. Now, those habits have evolved and are becoming more mainstream.

Consumer Trend Insights 2023 would like to call these consumers who use thrifty consumption strategies to make maximal use of their limited resources "Cherry-sumers." A "cherry picker" was a term with a slightly negative connotation, but in this book, "cherry" will be used broadly to denote any kind of "benefit," and the term "Cherry-sumer" will have a neutral sense. In recent years, the trend of thrifty consumption is slowly becoming a part of the culture among the younger crowd in Korean society. As the paradigm and methodology of consumption evolves with their emergence, Cherry-sumers, who satisfy their wants through meticulous selection given their limited resources, are changing the market.

The Cherry-sumer: Consumers' Shift to Recession Management

In the summer of 2022, a no-spending challenge, in which people do not spend a single penny a day, was a fad among twenty- and thirty-somethings. The key word here is "challenge," not "no-spending." Consumers these days have a different way of being frugal. They flaunt their spending history on social media or show off their saving tips. Instead of unboxing luxury goods on YouTube, they look up a video of, say, "unboxing an expense tracker" and participate in a "managing a household budget together" project using an app. In online communities, they write posts confessing, "I was able to make it without spending a single penny from Monday to Thursday, but I failed on Friday evening because I ordered fried chicken." They are also keen on the so-called "digital junk collection" trend where they receive points by signing into the app every day, or earn 140 won by walking 10,000 steps a day.

When the economy is bad, the spread of so-called "*jjan-tech*"짠테크 (a combination of the words for "being frugal" and for "investment technology") is a recurring trend. Consumers have always cut down spending in recessions. As mentioned in the introduction, a similar phenomenon occurred following the financial crisis in 2008. At that time, Cheil Worldwide제일기획 classified consumers along five different types. As the following table illustrates, consumers tend to adjust, reduce, or give up their purchases because real income and real purchasing power decrease during a recession. On the flipside, to find escape from prolonged

〈 Five Types of Consumers in Recessions (2008) 〉

Recession observer	Rather than just cutting spending, they watch the situation and make marginal adjustments. (forties, married, high-income group)
Recession cooperative	As the recession progresses, they reduce spending accordingly. (thirties and forties, middle-income group)
Recession controlled	They give up everything needed to help them get through the recession. (male, self-employed, low-income group)
Self-centered in the recession	They take the recession seriously but keep spending for themselves. (twenties, single)
Ignoring the recession	They maintain usual consumption patterns. (female, single, professional, high-income group)

Source: Cheil Worldwide (2009), Report on Consumer Types in Recessions 2009.

and restrained consumption, people indulge in buying "small luxuries."

15 years later, consumer behavior in 2023 is different from past recessions in many ways. In general, there are similarities in that spending has contracted, but in terms of individuals managing their expenditure, much has changed. The emergence of Cherry-sumers in 2023 can be expressed as the concurrent emergence of "recession management type" consumers, which have evolved from the five types mentioned above. Recession management consumers do not belong to one of these five types but are a "multi-persona" type of consumer who freely mix and use these five strategies according to the situation at hand to effectively manage the impact of the recession.

Rather than cutting down spending completely due to a decrease in real purchasing power, finding a suboptimal method and ways to save with other people is becoming the preferred choice. Recession management consumers satisfy their wants while using a spending strategy that makes maximal use of their limited resources. Also, apps and platforms that give wings to Cherry-sumers' consumer behavior are emerging. An environment that is positive towards the emergence of more Cherry-sumers is also helping. Smart consumers pursue rational and calculated consumption by sharing costs to get through the recession.

Cherry-sumers' consumption strategies can be divided

into three main categories. The first is a "divvying strategy." Instead of being bound by existing standards, they purchase only the amount they need and find savings in the process. The second is a "half-and-half strategy" which includes utilizing group purchasing. The third is a "flexi-strategy" which focuses on reducing risks that come from being bound by long-term contracts. Now, let's take a closer look at the new spending strategies of these thrifty Cherry-sumers.

Cherry-sumers' Three Consumption Strategies

1. Buying in pieces, the "divvying strategy"

A new policy implemented in June 2002 by the Ministry of Agriculture, Food and Rural Affairs that encourages the individual sale of agricultural products at large supermarkets makes it possible to buy just one color of paprika, rather than a bundle of yellow, red, and green ones. This policy has changed the way fresh food such as vegetables and fruits are sold by stacking them on shelves rather than packaging them separately. In line with the needs of today's consumers who want to purchase only what they need at the time rather than stockpiling large quantities, the ministry plans to further expand the items under coverage going forward.

Cherry-sumers' first strategy is "divvying up". Recently, consumers have begun to practice divvying up their purchases based on what is necessary for their lifestyle. The most common example of this can be found in supermarkets. Cherry-sumers prefer small packaging, despite the knowledge that bulk packaging is cheaper on a per unit or use basis. This preference is due to the lower price and the fact that no food is wasted. It is the opposite of the saying "the more the better." The rise in Cherry-sumers who prefer small packaging is evident in the data. According to Homeplus, among produce sold between June 1 to 15, 2022, the proportion of sales of "small packaging products" increased by 120% compared to January, and meat products also grew by 320%. For those who do not want to waste food, purchasing in small quantities is a more reasonable option than buying in bulk, even if the price per unit is slightly higher.

Cherry-sumers' love of small packaging has also led to a boom in convenience store shopping. Convenience stores that only sell simple foods such as rice rolls or lunch boxes are a thing of the past. A quarter of a head of cabbage for 900 won and two bundles of salad for 1,000 won are but two examples of what more people are shopping for at convenience stores – just enough fresh food to last them for a day or two. In response to this demand, the convenience store industry has also begun to stock a variety of fresh foods in small packaging. CU launched the "Singsing Saengsaeng싱싱생생" series, in which the vegetables that are most often used in Korean cuisine are sold in one or two small portions, as well as pork in smaller 200g portions. 7-Eleven also introduced "Seven Farm," a fresh food sub-brand consisting of offerings of one or two servings at a price comparable to that of large supermarkets.

Alcoholic beverages such as beer and wine are also popular in small quantities. Consumers who feel that 500ml is a little bit too much buy 250ml or 355ml sizes, which are easier to drink alone. The 250ml size soju, sold by Lotte Chilsung Beverage, has steadily increased in sales mainly at convenience stores, selling about 700 million bottles within three months of its launch, taking a strong position in the market. Along these lines, small-portion alcoholic beverages are gaining popularity, and new marketing attempts are being made offline. "Bottle Bunker," operated by Lotte Shopping, has had a positive reception as a paid wine "tasting tab" service that allows consumers to pay for just one glass at a time of a wide variety of wines classified by different themes. At the reasonable price of anywhere between 1,000 and 8,000 won per 50ml glass, consumers can "sip" their way through 80 different kinds of wine. It has attracted consumers who want to maximize their experiences with limited resources by paying for a glass of wine that is typically too expensive to try by the bottle.

The number of consumers who want to try out a variety of new products in small amounts through sample kits is also growing. In particular, the beauty industry is actively catching up to the trend by selling trial kits. If you do a search for "sample kit" or "miniature set," sample kits from various cosmetic brands such as Sulwhasoo, Isoi, and Etude House pop up. Cherry-sumers have been attracted to the prospect of being able to experience an entire line, from toners to serums and cream, for a week at a much lower price than that of full-sized products. More recently, "experience kits" are being offered for items beyond cosmetics, from fabric softeners to dog treats. It can be a bit much to purchase the full-sized product, so it offers another alternative to cherry-sumers who want to just try out a product.

In Japan, a business model of splitting up home rentals has emerged. Rerent Residence Shibuya, a Japanese shared-housing brand, garnered popularity for its plan that reduces monthly rents by the number of days the rented room was left vacant. Located three minutes from Shibuya Station in Tokyo, the monthly rent for a fully furnished 36m² room is about 2 million won when converted to Korean currency. The rent is not cheap. However, there is a secret hidden in this plan: if the tenant doesn't stay in the room, the monthly rent will be cut down. If a tenant applies to vacate the room three days in advance through an app, the vacant room is leased out to the public as a hotel room to make a profit, and a portion of the profit is returned to the occupant. The monthly rent is discounted at about 6,000 yen per day (about 60,000 Korean won), and the room can be vacated for up to 15 days. It is the emergence of a new housing culture in which users pay for and use housing as much as they need it, when they need it.

Consumers these days are even enjoying luxury products by splitting them into pieces. As mentioned earlier, sales of "small luxury" items, which can serve as a pick-me-up when having a bad day, tend to increase rather than completely taper off during a recession. The emerging trend is consumers splitting small luxury items into, well, "tiny luxury" items. The "vintage luxury button accessory" trend, which is popular among Gen Z, is an interesting example. Instead of purchasing high-end accessories directly from the store, they purchase products that have been upcycled into accessories such as earrings and necklaces. These are made by attaching materials to vintage buttons from luxury clothing. In Korea, selling luxury buttons such as "Chanel Buttons" and "Louis Vuitton Buttons" through second-hand trading platforms is trending. Depending on the design and color, six to seven pieces are typically sold at about 400,000-700,000 won. This tiny luxury trend is a prime example of Cherry-sumers' divvying strategy, which splits up and consumes luxury goods even with limited resources.

2. Buying together and the "half-half strategy"

There are some things that people want to buy that are either too expensive or difficult to split up. In this case,

Cherry-sumers actively search for someone to share the costs and benefits with.

An example is "delivery fee splitting" which was introduced in the media in early 2022. When a driver went out for a food delivery, he was surprised to find a large number of residents all waiting together for the same delivery. More and more residents are ordering food deliveries together to save on the rising delivery fees. The method is simple: one person posts "Who wants Chinese food?" in an open chat room and two or three households who want to order from the same menu participate, each ordering the food they want and then splitting the delivery fee.

Cherry-sumers who actively use the half-half strategy can often be found on social media and in the used goods market. In order to facilitate splitting costs, they divide up and resell bulk products on social media or second-hand trading apps. Or they purchase such pre-divided products themselves. The types of items that are bought and sold include everything from notepads and perfumes to detergent. In the case of cosmetics, food, and health supplements, the number of related posts is increasing rapidly reflecting rising inflation, despite the fact that sales of these specific items are prohibited on second-hand trading platforms under current law. In the past, some might ask, "Is it really necessary to go that far?" But for Cherry-sumers, this type of splitting-up and selling activity is more of a game that provides entertainment, going beyond just cutting costs. In July 2022, Daangn Market당근마켓 launched the "Buy Together" service where neighbors gather to buy and split up their purchases, reflecting growing consumer demand. Neighbors gather to buy a good or service by, for example, posting or responding to the post "Who will buy and split a box of apples with me" on the app.

As group purchasing habits spread, the related platform industry has boomed. The concept of group purchasing, which is simply several people gathering to buy a product at a discount, is a purchasing method that has been around for ages. The first generation of group purchasers, which started with Groupon in the United States in 2008, was a method in which a platform or influencer recruited group buyers, and when a certain threshold of buyers was reached, the group could purchase together at a discounted price. But now this method is evolving into a more flexible and consumer-oriented business model. For example, Always올웨이즈, a platform developed by a startup launched in 2021, has racked up over 1 million members within five months of its launch by streamlining the sales method. The platform allows purchases at a discounted price if the target number of people is reached within a certain time. If the target number of people is not reached, the buyers are automatically refunded, allowing buyers to purchase products easily and cost effectively with family members or acquaintances. It is perfect for Cherry-sumers who are pursuing a divvying strategy, as well.

Platforms that find people who will pay certain fees together are also attracting Cherry-sumers. This resolves the problem of trying to find someone to split the bill with, as well as the hassle of settling the bill, helping maximize utility at minimal cost. Apps that find someone with whom to share delivery fees (which have become pricey to pay for on one's own); platforms that support sharing video streaming subscription accounts; platforms that connect people together to taxi-pool to the same destination – all of these are in line with Cherry-sumers' half-half strategy. For example, the Pickle Plus피클플러스 app lets users find other users with whom to sign up for video streaming subscription plans such as Netflix and Watcha through the "Party Matching" function. In addition, it provides a function that automatically rematches new members to a subscription group when one of the members leaves. This service has racked up over 200,000 subscribers.

3. Buying flexibly, the "flexi-strategy"

Another Cherry-sumer strategy is the "flexi- strategy." Rather than becoming tied to a long-term contract and paying a fixed amount each month, the strategy is to ensure flexibility by signing up for a service only for as long as the service is needed. The goal is to offer buyers freedom by strategically managing their spending through flexible contracts that can be canceled easily. Flexible contract terms often require additional costs relative to long-term contracts, but Cherry-sumers do not hesitate to pay up, favoring flexibility that affords control over the terms of the contract.

As more consumers seek contractual flexibility, many industries are starting to come up with policies to cater to this demand. First, the flexi-strategy in the subscription economy is one of the key examples. Consumers in their twenties and thirties, who find the cost of fixed monthly payments a burden, have started a "subscription fee diet." They cancel subscription services that they no longer use as much, and then use an on-demand payment strategy to keep a subscription only when needed. Existing subscription services have until now focused on finding ways to offer benefits such as cost-effectiveness and new experiences, and cherry-sumers have added "flexible management" as an additional requirement.

The subscription service Suldamhwa술담화, which delivers traditional Korean liquor selected by a sommelier, features a "take a break" function: if the drink of the month does not seem interesting, or if there is still some undrunk alcohol at home, users can skip a delivery without paying a fee. It may not be good for the company's sales, but it has garnered good feedback by catering to consumers' lifestyles, encouraging them to maintain their subscriptions. LG U⁺

and SKT, which recently introduced integrated subscription services, are also moving towards offering more convenience in subscription management. The subscription service platform Yudok유독 launched by LG U⁺ has gotten rid of extra fees and inconvenient cancellations. This feature allows consumers to choose and subscribe only to the services they want according to their lifestyle and to change to a different service every month. SKT's T Universe has also increased flexibility so that consumers can choose the subscription plan that suits them best by being able to add features they want to their basic plans. As a result, it racked up 1.2 million users within the first ten months of the service's launch. These two services are also easier to cancel than in the past, making progress in moving away from the "easy to join but difficult to leave" model of telecommunication companies in the past, keeping up with new customer trends.

Cherry-sumers are also looking for more effective ways to deal with high insurance premiums that require consistent, long-term payments. As a result, the insurance industry is launching a "mini-insurance" product in which users sign up for a relatively short period when they need insurance, paying only for what they use. It is a low-cost, short-term insurance that reduces premiums for a limited period of around one year, and a growing number of products have been developed since the amendment of the Insurance Business Act introduced new short-term insurance plans effective from June 2021. For example, Carrot Insurance introduced "per mile auto insurance," where users pay premiums only for their actual mileage. It also introduced the industry's first deferred payment calculation system. Traditional car insurance meant users have to pay a fixed amount every year, regardless of how much they use the car. Carrot introduced deferred payment insurance that calculates exactly the distance traveled per month, targeting consumers in their twenties and thirties – many of whom think insurance premiums are a waste. This new type of insurance is very popular among Cherry-sumers, as can be seen in the figures: the cumulative number of Carrot's subscribers surpassed 700,000 in just two years since its launch.

The travel industry is adapting too. Up until now, penalties have been accepted as a normal travel cost in cases where customers have to cancel their travel reservations. However, as more Cherry-sumers want a more flexible contract that can be easily canceled, the industry has begun to address the demand. The pandemic has further accelerated the trend. Although demand for travel has increased after the lifting of social distancing measures, the industry is implementing new strategies to attract consumers who still have cold feet. For example, Coupang Travel쿠팡트래블 has broken with convention by introducing a "100% money-back guarantee" policy that gives a full refund even if users cancel just one day before the hotel reservation date. Travel agency

Modetour모두투어 also launched a product that waives the penalty fees for overseas travel reservations in consideration of rapidly changing travel restrictions. Furthermore, Airbnb has introduced a refund policy search filter so that users can easily find and book accommodations that have a flexible refund policy. This option provides a full refund if users cancel even up to one day before check-in. The travel industry is in a race to adapt to the changing needs of Cherry-sumers.

Background:
Why YOLO Consumers Look for Cherries, Too

Deteriorating economy and the era of "one-economy 2.0"

The reason for Cherry-sumers' emergence is, above all, the deterioration of the economy. It is the unprecedented threat of inflation and economic instability that has led even younger generations, who used to live by the mantras "YOLO" (You Only Live Once) and "Flex" (showing off), to start looking for deals. According to a 2021 Korea Economic Research Institute analysis of "perceived economic pain" indexed by generation, economic hardships were felt most strongly among young adults in the 15-29 age group. The perceived economic pain index is an index adapted from American economist Arthur Okun's "misery index" and is calculated by combining the perceived unemployment rate and the inflation rate by age group. As consumer prices and

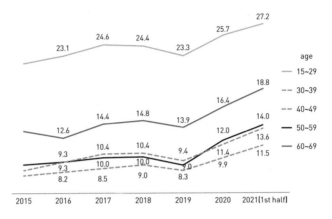

〈 Perceived Economic Pain Index 〉

23.1	24.6	24.4		23.3	25.7	27.2

age
— 15~29
-- 30~39
-- 40~49
— 50~59
— 60~69

12.6	14.4	14.8	13.9		16.4	18.8
9.3	10.4	10.4	9.4	12.0		14.0
9.3	10.0	10.0	9.0	11.4	13.6	11.5
8.2	8.5	9.0	8.3	9.9		

| 2015 | 2016 | 2017 | 2018 | 2019 | 2020 | 2021(1st half) |

Source: Korea Economic Research Institute

the unemployment rate of 15- to 29-year-olds in Korea surge, the economic challenges are only intensifying. The one way young people can overcome these difficulties is to become a Cherry-sumer and make maximal use of their limited resources.

The Cherry-sumer trend is also a result of structural changes in which single-person households become mainstream and they prefer smaller and more flexible consumption. When the keyword "one-economy ¹코노미" was introduced in *Consumer Trend Insights 2017*, the percentage of single-person households in Korea was at 27.2%. Since then, that proportion has gone up to 40.3%, exceeding

40% for the first time, according to the *2022 Administrative Safety Statistical Yearbook* released by the Ministry of Public Administration and Security. This means while the total population has decreased, the number of registered households has actually increased by 1.6%. The era of "one-economy 2.0," which is dominated by single-person households, has officially begun.

Low-cost, high-efficiency spending is done more easily in large families because economies of scale also work for households. The bigger the household, the lower the per capita expenditure. For example, there is no need to buy items that are used together, such as TVs, refrigerators, and washing machines. If four people use a refrigerator that costs 1 million won, the cost per person would be 250,000 won. On the other hand, single-person households must purchase a TV, refrigerator, and washing machine on their own – this is an example of economies of scale at work in domestic spending. Expenditure management for single-person households is therefore much more difficult than for larger households. Therefore, Cherry-sumers must actively manage spending in a way that is optimized for one person. If they are not careful, they may easily fall into the trap of overspending. This means that the one-economy consumers, who enjoyed small and flexible consumption as a necessity rather than as a lifestyle choice, are now also evolving into a form of Cherry-sumers in the face of the economic downturn.

The first generation poorer than their parents gets creative

Generation MZ, the core generation of Cherry-sumers, was born into a low-growth period and is known as the "first generation that is poorer than their parents." They grew up hearing the saying, "If you work hard, you can achieve anything," and have impeccable qualifications. Yet, as they become adults, it is difficult for them to afford their own houses. On the other hand, since they were children, they have been exposed to many experiences, so their standards are high. For this group of people who live a life full of wants but have limited resources, meticulous financial management is a natural development.

Spending patterns of MZ consumers are frequently described with keywords such as "YOLO" and "Flex." But looking only at these keywords can be misleading. This generation is just as well known for their rational consumption choices as other generations are. As a generation with good self-management skills, they are also skilled at managing expenses. Jeon In-goo, a popular finance YouTuber in his thirties, said in an interview, "when it comes to *jjan-tech* (savvy, frugal spending), many say that eating at home rather than eating out is the right economical choice, but I eat out and just work more with that time and energy – I'm a time-saver." With the knowledge that buying cheap is not always the best answer, he tries to find a balance between his current economic situation and his needs. Generation MZ, which has a strong grasp of capitalism and is experienced with managing spending, is accelerating the expansion of Cherry-sumers.

Cherry-sumers are not passive. They don't give up their wants unconditionally or cut down spending just because of a lack of resources. Instead of giving in to the current situation they manage wants by deriving creative solutions, either on their own or with others. Consumption methods such as buying and drinking only one glass of wine instead of a bottle or sharing video streaming account subscriptions to divvy up costs with others, are all examples of Cherry-sumerism.

Outlook and Implications

Some will view the emergence of Cherry-sumers as a temporary change while consumers cope with an economic downturn. But given the ongoing trend in managing consumption amid the growing number of single-person households, it is likely to be a trend that will continue even once the economy bounces back in the future. So, how should companies adapt to Cherry-sumerism? If companies used to view Cherry-sumers as a small group of consumers trying to cut corners amid a recession, they will now need to upend that stereotype. It would also be a mistake to classify them as black "consumers from hell" just looking for freebies, or to overlook them as consumers only looking for quick deals. At the same time, overdoing discounts is not the answer either. As the number of Cherry-sumers who want smaller portions and more flexible spending options increases, it is time to devise an appropriate strategy to match.

In social psychology, there is a term called the "foot-in-the-door" technique. It is a strategy first coined in 1966 by psychologists Jonathan Freedman and Scott Fraser, in which one gets a smaller request granted before making a larger request. It is a persuasion technique that makes it easier to get people to comply with requests.

How about applying this technique to Cherry-sumers? Companies could provide the option for consumers to experience a specific product with a small sample or to try out a service for a short period of time. As Cherry-sumers become more familiar with the brand, they help increase brand recognition which can then lead to further interest in the brand's other products. That quick experience can work to break down the psychological barrier for first timers and open the door for consumers to purchase full-sized prod-ucts. For example, premium fragrance brand Tamburins탬버린즈 took advantage of the growing number of Cherry-sum-ers. They categorize fragrance sample kits based on price, between 3,000 and 5,000 won. During the pandemic, people were skeptical and asked, "Who is going to pay for samples?" However, conventional stereotypes about samples were broken. The company started selling samples in a well-designed package using a tin case. As a result, buyers posted reviews on social media with positive responses such as, "How can sample kits look so nice?" and "This is totally my style." The new product was sold out within three days of its launch. The special brand experience offered by the small sample succeeded in getting Cherry-sumers to start spending.

This is not just limited to new brands and startups. Larger companies also need a strategy to increase brand recognition by establishing a lower-end product line. Samsung Electronics has recently launched the entry-level, low-priced Galaxy A23 5G model and is trying to bring Cherry-sumers onboard. With the Galaxy S and Galaxy Z series, the company targets the premium market while expanding the scope of smartphones with cost-effective product lines. The emergence of Cherry-sumers should be seen as an opportunity to increase brand recognition and to build a more diverse product ecosystem.

The virtues of a well-mannered consumer

The role consumers play has been diversifying. Consumers are purchasers, users, allocators of their own limited resources, and recently, they even play the role of influencers and creators that inspire new products to hit the market. As the power of consumers grows, the responsibilities that they have are becoming increasingly important.

The inappropriate behavior of a handful of consumers that borders on the illegal has been raising concerns. Some ignore the contract signed with a company, resell parts of a service, or even find loopholes to use the product or service without paying the full price. Such actions infringe on the interests of the vast majority of consumers and may leave a negative effect on the broader market and industry. The term "ignorance challenge" has appeared as people criticize the excessive actions of certain consumers that engage in inappropriate behaviors such as making a meal out of company pantry snacks. Being frugal is good, but consumer ethics also need to be considered. Consumers have an obligation to comply with contracts and should not disrupt market order in an attempt to maximize the effectiveness of their own limited resources.

Consumers have more influence on the market than ever before. As the recession progresses, Cherry-sumers should think about consumer ethics while they manage their spending. As the nation's economy looks for new ways to weather the recession, it is time for consumers and businesses to work together to create a more efficient market.

Buddies with a Purpose:

'Index Relationships'

As communication mediums evolve, the nature of relationships changes along with them. Where "establishing relationships" in the past consisted in forming close friendships with a small number of people, today's relationships are better characterized as a result of "relationship management" with a focus on maximizing efficiency by indexing different types of relationships based on their purpose. *Consumer Trend Insights 2023* would like to name this trend "Index Relationships" to draw attention to recent trends in personal relationships that take this form of relationship management via the attaching of various index labels.

Index Relationships consist of three stages: creation, categorization, and management. The formation of relationships is no longer as dependent on naturally formed connections, such as academic or personal ties, as it was in the past, but is rather dependent on connections formed either intentionally with a clear purpose, or in a completely random way by chance. As the media through which people communicate with one another has become more variegated, the degrees of intimacy in relationships have become just as complicated. In other words, as the importance of relationships is constructed in multiple dimensions rather than by a single criterion, the "relationship spectrum" has become more important than the "depth of a relationship." The last stage consists of actively managing the created and classified relationships by attaching and detaching index labels as the nature of the connection evolves. As our society shifts towards individualism and navigates through a pandemic that has completely changed the way we socialize, it is only natural that the pattern of relationship building changes accordingly. Massive change is happening in what is no doubt the most important aspect of human history: personal relationships. Now, the question is, in a society where these various indexes and methods of classification crisscross between us, how can we build happier relationships?

W hat's worse: having your message "left on read" (receiver reads the message but does not reply) or having it "left unread" (receiver doesn't even read the message)? This regularly occurring situation has been a key point of contention in online debates. Some say being "left on read" is better since it clearly states the receiver's intention to decline engagement. Others prefer the "left unread" side as it implies the receiver is too busy to open the message, meaning the sender has not been ignored outright. Which side do you prefer?

The choice will ultimately be a matter of personal preference. The point is that people are making assumptions regarding another person's intentions, going so far as to evaluate a relationship based on the time it takes to read and respond to messages. The way one replies to a KakaoTalk message is just out of personal habit, so why is it interpreted so severely as the measure of the depth of a relationship? This highlights how complex and diverse today's relationships have become compared to the past, making it more difficult to understand them.

This complexity is particularly true with today's friendships. In the days of the landline telephone, your friends were just the people you listed in a notebook. But now, the endless social platforms such as KakaoTalk, Facebook, Instagram, and the metaverse each offer different types of relationships. Furthermore, relationships in modern society no longer fall in the simple dichotomy of "close / not close," but have become much more complex. Instagram friends인친 who inspire you; Twitter friends트친 who share the same interests and follow the same celebrities as you; Facebook friends페친 who update you on the latest news; and "real" friends실친 you meet in your neighborhood – they are all part of a very diverse spectrum that exists within the single word "friend." Amid these constantly evolving relationships, people are trying to infer how one's counterpart defines a relationship by reading between the lines, or between the messages – picking up on any hints or cues in how the friend replies to text messages.

An index is a list in which data is recorded, with items such as name, number, size, attributes, location, etc., displayed in a table. In this vein, the complex relationships in modern society are now managed by attaching an index label to each connection. While close friendships with a small number of people have characterized the essence of what constitutes "establishing relationships" in the past, today's relationships are better defined as a result of "relationship management" with a focus on maximizing efficiency by indexing different relationship types based on their purpose. We would like to name this trend of strategically formed and managed relationships "Index Relationships."

Index Relationships consist of three stages: creation, categorization, and management. Here, the process of creating a new relationship is different from the traditional way. Rather than expecting relationships to be created naturally in everyday life, people actively seek out relationships with the purpose of building a wider network, or seek out encounters with people who are otherwise difficult to meet in daily life. Through this process the "pool" from which new relationships are created can be extended indefinitely. Second, after a relationship is created, it is classified through an indexing process based on levels of closeness. Relationships that are no longer necessary are quietly cut off and blocked, while intimate relationships are characterized with a level of sharing private details that some may see as excessive. Third, these classifications for each relationship are not fixed but rather are managed efficiently by continuously attaching and removing index labels as the relationship evolves. Maintaining good relationships also requires a corresponding strategy. Maintaining an appropriate distance so that the other counterpart feels neither burdened nor disappointed is key. Let us analyze the characteristics of Index Relationships in detail to better understand the new patterns in relationship formation.

Three Stages of Index Relationships

1. Creating relationships: Don't rely solely on personal ties

How are human relationships created? Take, for example, your best friend and think about the moment you first met. How did you become friends? Most relationships start off naturally by chance. Having the same major, being in the same class, social club, hobby group, or hanging out among colleagues are some of the common ways people meet in everyday life which don't require any special effort. Relationships in modern society, however, no longer rely solely on chance encounters. Building a relationship requires intention and effort. Such effort helps to expand the pool of relationships beyond what natural and chance encounters are able to do.

The first type of Index Relationship is the "purpose-driven relationship." This refers to a relationship formed with a clear purpose in mind. Extracurricular activities that college students participate in these days is an example of the shift. There is a gradual move in interest away from social clubs to academic clubs, and, further, from academic clubs to entrepreneurship clubs – a shift toward groups that have clearer purposes. College students in the past participated in club activities to meet friends from other majors and enjoy hobbies. Finding a job now has become more challenging amid intensifying competition, and the number of students participating in social clubs has gradually fallen. Instead, academic clubs have grown in popularity as they can beef up a résumé. More recently, students have gravitated toward activities with a clear purpose, such as entrepreneurship clubs to help found a start-up. It is no longer about meeting new people and doing new things but about setting out to expand social networks while also doing something new in the process.

One of the areas where purpose-driven relationships are most evident is the dating scene. The younger generations these days fret that "dating is becoming increasingly challenging." Tales from their parents' generation where they, for example, "ran into each other in the library and fell in love at first sight," are now a thing of the past. This trend has been further amplified by the pandemic as virtual relationships replaced many real-life relationships. Thus, the current generation has become more familiar with meeting someone through more artificial encounters, rather than natural ones. Meeting someone with a clear intention to pursue a relationship is now seen as the shortcut to successful matchups.

Public posts announcing "self-promoted blind dates셀소" are frequent on social platforms widely used by college students, such as the meeting and blind date bulletin boards of Everytime에타 and the college student community-centered Campus Pick캠퍼스픽. It works like a classified ad: you introduce yourself with your age, personality, hobbies, and your ideal type, and if a match happens to read your post, they may ask you out on a date. Sometimes, a third person takes on the role of matchmaker. This is also known as a "Madam-Ting마담팅" – a mash-up of a type of matchmaker in Korea, "Madam Tu마담뚜," and the word for "blind date소개팅" – because a third party sets up a meeting by matching men and women who are suitable for each other based on the information they have shared. Self-promoted blind dates are popular not only among college students but also among office workers, as evidenced on the anonymous community platform Blind. There was a total of 110,000 posts on the topic of self-promoted blind dates on Blind in 2021, doubling from 55,000 in 2019. The number of dating app users with the express purpose of meeting people online has also increased significantly. As of December 2021, the number of domestic dating app users increased by 55.3% compared to the previous year, according to App Ape, a mobile market research service.

Even when it comes to marriage, purpose-driven relationships are an emerging trend. According to matchmaking agency Duo듀오, its members increased by around 22% in 2021 from the previous year. As opportunities to meet new dating partners through blind dates and clubs dwindled during and in the aftermath of the pandemic, the number of single men and women looking for matchmaking services with the goal of getting married has surged. "In the past, it was the parents who came to sign up for their children's memberships, but after the pandemic the number of unmarried men and women who joined voluntarily is growing," said Duo CEO Park Soo-kyung. It is notable that among the current generation, who would seem to prefer a freer dating style over matchmaking, more and more are choosing to use these services with the purpose of getting married.

The purpose-driven relationship trend stands out even further when it comes to hobbies. Unlike the parents' generation, where neighborhood acquaintances might gather for a game of soccer, the younger generations meet people based on topics of interest, such as mountain climbing, snorkeling, art exhibitions, or musical performances. Take Frip프립 for example: a social activity platform where a host creates a meeting with a specific topic and users pay a fee to participate in the activity. People with various interests gather to learn skills, like coding, or to share in their hobbies, such as hiking while listening to music or taking a walk along the Fortress Wall of Seoul. The purpose takes precedence over the relationship.

The second type of Index Relationship is the so-called "random relationship." A random relationship is a method of expanding networks by intentionally creating an accidental encounter with a stranger for whom it would be otherwise difficult to find a naturally occurring intersection point. Random relationships focus on fleeting entertainment. Therefore, rather than the goal of cultivating a long-term relationship with someone, the random relationship is characterized by fulfilling the need of a moment, whether it be entertainment or information, which is then quickly discarded. Among iPhone users the popular "Airdrop game" is one such example. AirDrop is Apple's proprietary file transfer protocol that can quickly and wirelessly transfer photos, videos, and other files between devices over a nine-meter range. The Airdrop game uses these features to exchange entertaining videos with strangers in the vicinity.

Random chat rooms are also popular among Generation Z. Online random video chat website Omegle launched in the US in 2009 toting the slogan "Talk to strangers!" This forgotten platform was made relevant again because of the function it offered for users to find common interests. By entering a keyword of interest and clicking the chat button, a chat room opens with another randomly chosen user who has chosen the same interest. This service's differentiating factor lies in the fact that users can focus more on sharing common interests than on wasting time with small talk over personal information and perfunctory greetings, as is the case with most online chatting services.

The popularity of random "open" chat rooms, where users can communicate with a group of strangers, is also growing rapidly. A Gen Z favorite, the "YouTube Casual Chatroom유튜브 반모방," is a channel where users exchange casual chit-chat with no set topic as they would with close friends in the channel's comment window. Users can open videos and share personal stories. Invitations are made using a link, and when the chat session is over, the room disappears for good. KakaoTalk has also expanded from being solely an "acquaintance-centered" communication network to a broader community-based platform. The number of users is growing on the platform's Open Chat function, a Kakao chat room where strangers that share the same interests can gather without needing to add one another as a friend. The number of open chat users in 2022 has grown by about 76% compared to 2019, accounting for about 40% of the total conversation volume, according to Kakao figures. Kakao sees the popularity of open chatting as "a reflection of the characteristics of today's generation, which avoids engaging with other people more than necessary," and expects the platform to evolve into one that goes well beyond communicating with personal acquaintances only.

2. Categorizing relationships: Indexing by importance

In the past, defining a "friend" was straightforward. How often one meets a friend was typically the determining factor for how close the relationship was. You would go to class, lunch, and club activities with close friends. A best friend could be a confidant who listens to your private concerns, a buddy who pulls all-nighters with you, or a partner who indulges in the same hobbies as you. True friendships existed offline, while online relationships were just fleeting encounters.

Compared with the past, defining a "close relationship" is now much more complicated. Data from a Gen Z relationship analysis workshop conducted by Seoul National University's Consumer Trend Analysis Center found that Gen Zers classified relationships in which they share their study sessions with a study buddy in real time over Zoom, and other online relationships conducted mainly through social media, as being closer relationships than those with friends they met once or twice a year in an offline setting. Offline relationships no longer take precedence over their online counterparts.

How did this result come to be? The reason is that the criteria by which people determine the closeness of relationships has become more complex compared with the past. Face-to-face meetings were important when online and offline relationships were clearly defined and assigned corresponding importance, but today, when relationships can easily be maintained in a multitude of ways, face-to-face meetings are just one of the many ways to cultivate a relationship. Online and offline relationships now intersect with each other, creating a whole new set of relationship types. The relationships of modern society have become so complex they now must be expressed as falling on a "relationship

⟨Relationship Intimacy Defined by Generation Z⟩

Degree of Intimacy		Example
Very close	Real-time sharing of private life	- Turn on videoconferencing program such as Zoom and share your daily life: "Study With Me" - Share real-time location on social media: Zenly
Close	Constant communication	- Phone calls - Kakao Talk: personal chats - Social network services: sending and receiving direct messages (DM) - Meeting: once every two or three months
Somewhat close	Information updates	- Communicate through blogs: adding neighbors to friends lists - Social network services: tagging, liking, scrolling - Kakao Talk: open chat rooms
Acquaintance	Status updates	- Meeting: once or twice a year

Source: Seoul National University Consumer Trend Analysis Center, Research Data on Generation Z, 2022.

spectrum" where multiple reference points intersect rather than just lying on a single axis of a relationship's depth or level of intimacy.

As relationships become more complex, people have started indexing different social network platforms by assigning certain roles to them. Teenagers typically use KakaoTalk for relatively serious situations, such as "discussing a team project for school" or when "having an argument with a friend." Therefore, some teenagers get anxious when they receive a KakaoTalk message from a friend as they assume it is about a serious topic. For lighter daily updates, Facebook or Instagram is used to share direct messages (DMs). On these platforms DMs with a specific purpose such as quick messages asking "Where are you?" or "What's up?" are more common, suggesting they serve as a more daily and casual medium compared to KakaoTalk. This is also shown by the fact that people choose to talk about work with managers through KakaoTalk rather than by DMs on Facebook or Instagram.

This shift is apparent in the numbers. Only 54% of teenage respondents chose KakaoTalk as the app they mostly use to communicate with friends and acquaintances, according to a survey by mobile research firm Consumer Insight. This is quite lower than the rate of KakaoTalk preference among other age groups, which was over 80%. The gap is also apparent (though in the opposite direction) in the percentage of teenagers using Facebook messages: 31%, but only 1-4% in other age groups. Just like relationships are indexed by criteria such as "homework buddies," "friends to discuss concerns," and "hobby mates," social media platforms are also differentiated by these index labels.

Even within the same platforms, different relationship indexes exist. If the relationship is not important, it can be indexed with a "block" tag. Others may post a status display message with "Replies may be delayed" on KakaoTalk, letting messages pile up and avoiding reading them in order to distance themselves from certain people. And sometimes the actual blocking function of the platform is used. The "close friends" setting on Instagram is a feature that allows only people on an approved list to be able to see story updates. Messaging service WhatsApp offers customized functions for users to prevent themselves from being added to chatrooms by certain people.

On the other end of the spectrum, a "sasaeng사생" index label is attached to extremely close friends with whom even the most minute and personal details of one's daily life are shared. Zenly, a location sharing app that shows icons of people on a map, allows friends to check each other's current location, movement direction and speed, and even a friend's remaining phone battery life. Because of this, Zenly users say, "Lying doesn't work on Zenly." For example, since real-time location information is shared, it is easy to check whether a friend will be arriving to a meetup on time. The battery and sleep status displays mean small lies such as "my battery died" or "I fell asleep while talking" no longer work. Real-time notifications also pop up when other friends on your list are meeting up.

3. Maintaining relationships: Manage them strategically

The final characteristic of Index Relationships is "relationship management." People strategically manage their classified relationships by constantly attaching and detaching index labels. In order to maintain numerous relationships within a complex "relationship spectrum," a shrewd relationship maintenance strategy is required – one that allows people to avoid spending unnecessary resources on each other while also keeping an appropriate distance.

"Relationship cleanup" is the first step in managing relationships. After the indexing of complex relationships is complete, unnecessary relationships require periodic "cleaning up." In Japan, "relationship reset syndrome," which consists of clearing out relationships to relieve the stress caused by unnecessary personal ties, has recently become a growing trend. Like a reset button reboots an overloaded computer, rather than forcing a match with everyone, people end some relationships and redirect resources to start a new one. These resets include everything from deleting a social media account and creating a fresh one, deleting all phone contacts, to even changing jobs or moving homes without updating acquaintances. Similar trends to minimize relationship stress are apparent in Korea as well. According to a survey conducted by Job Korea and Albamon in 2020, about 87.1% of 1,409 adults responded that a "social diet" was needed to clean up unnecessary personal relationships, such as deleting social media accounts or changing phone numbers.

Once the cleanup is complete, the key is to then exert effort on strategically maintaining your remaining relationships. With casual acquaintances, it is important to keep ties at a distance so as not to create unnecessary stress. Frequent in-person meetings are not a necessity in the realm of Index Relationships. This is made possible because today's younger generation can build and cultivate relationships in a multitude of ways, without face-to-face interaction. Social media platforms reduce the awkwardness that comes from long periods of time spent physically apart. Even without communicating often, status updates on social media disclose more than enough daily details with one's connections. Simply liking, commenting, or replying to a friend's Instagram story or post allows people to maintain relationships over long periods of time at a comfortable distance and without unnecessary pressure.

The types of tools available for communication and relationship management are also becoming more diverse. Friends are sharing the most minute details about their lives through mediums such as shared virtual notepads and calendars. For example, an office worker in her 30s who enjoys trying out new Michelin-rated restaurants organizes a list of restaurants she has recently visited on a smartphone notepad and shares it with close friends. There is no particular greeting or message on the notepad – just a list of when and where she ate lunch or dinner. There is no feedback either. The sole act of sharing a list of common interests conveys the depth of a given relationship.

Sharing one's personal itineraries is another way to signal

closeness in a relationship. Todo Mate is a checklist-oriented scheduling app that helps track daily to-do list items. Gen Zers use the sharing feature of this productivity app as they would any other social media platform. By adding a friend in the app, they are able to view the other person's schedule for the day and receive notifications on whether the other person has completed the day's tasks. Handwriting app GoodNotes is another example of an app being used as a social communication platform. It offers a function to share user-created templates for others to use which then serves as its own social media platform. For example, if users create a "diary template" and send the link to each other, they can peek into each other's diaries. Through something as simple as clicking "share my diary" users are able to keep tabs on each other's lives without daily phone calls.

The easiest way to convey that you want to continue a relationship with someone is by "gifting." KakaoTalk's gifting function is popular among those in their 20s. To keep in touch without frequent communication, sending a gift card on anniversaries and birthdays to simply say "I'm thinking of you," is common. The gifting function also makes keeping tabs easy, with past gift exchanges being automatically saved in the app's history. If someone sent a present on a friend's birthday, it would be polite to reciprocate. And if that friend failed to reciprocate come the gift-sender's birthday, the relationship would naturally come to an end.

Background to Index Relationships

Why have Index Relationships become such an increasingly prevalent phenomenon in our lives? Changes in relationships are directly correlated with changes in the tools used to communicate. The days of contacting acquaintances by phone or text message has given way to an era of communicating with the general public through social media. With that, the number of relationships we have to manage also increased exponentially. The medium has effectively changed its essence. As communication mediums evolve, the nature of relationships changes with them. In order to understand the background of the emergence of Index Relationships, it is necessary to understand the correlative links between evolving communication mediums and personal relationships.

Redefinition of relationship caused by the pandemic

The pandemic has forced us to reassess the definition of a personal relationship. When alone at home during social distancing, the only relationships people had access to were those that had already been established. To create a new relationship, the only available options were online communities and social network platforms where people could communicate anonymously. A social media analysis by Konan Technology of keywords related to "personal relationships," "friendship," "friends," and "best friends," shows that searches for keywords related to social distancing such as "Instagram" and "mobile phone" rose during 2021 when the pandemic was at its peak and again in the first half of 2022 amidst a resurgence of the virus.

In his recent book *Friends: Understanding the Power of Our Most Important Relationships,* British cultural anthropologist Robin Dunbar states that online social networks are places where people interact with offline friends and are not where new friends are made. Facebook is merely a communication tool, as phone calls were to our grandparents' generation, and nothing more. Friends can be made online, though rarely, and most people just add friends that they already know on online platforms, he says. Yet, the unprecedented changes brought on by the pandemic may have served as the decisive opportunity to prove this assertion incorrect. During times of lockdown and social distancing, the proposition that "online relationships can exist on their own" proved itself as a replacement of "online relationships merely supplement relationships in real life."

What is also clear is that even despite the pandemic, the number of Index Relationships in our lives was already growing rapidly. The new norms of modern society and changing expectations towards personal relationships have collided with the emergence of Index Relationships. In that regard, it is crucial to understand why people are no longer fully served by existing relationship patterns, and why they are looking to adopt new Index Relationships.

First, in the context of Index Relationships, the question is what is behind the emergence of "purpose-driven relationships" – whether it be a specific relationship created with an end goal in mind, or a random relationship that helps expand one's network? The answer lies largely in the fact that the lives of people in modern society no longer follow the same life stages as that of their friends. In the past, when society was relatively homogeneous, friends of the same age groups experienced school, employment, marriage, and childbirth at more or less the same time. In contrast, these days, life cycles are different even among friends of the same age. There are friends in their 30s who are married with children, while others are still enjoying the single life. That naturally cuts down on opportunities to share information about common topics.

This is where online networks fill in the information gaps. Information related to job searches, marriage, childbirth, and parenting is shared through internet communities and public chat rooms. Instead of turning to that best friend with one's personal worries, gathering answers to questions in the comments by posting about one's concerns on an online message board has become the norm. In this respect, "purpose-driven relationships" and "random relationships" that help expand the pool of relationships have become more in line with the needs and expectations of people today.

More self-centered perspectives of relationships

Second, in the context of classifying and maintaining Index Relationships, why do people use dynamic indexes for relationships and strategically manage them? This is due to a shift toward more self-centered perspectives of relationships. Today, people generally put themselves first, and do not get hung up on the minutiae of personal relationships. In the past, enduring and maintaining uncomfortable relationships was considered a virtue. Today, these trying relationships are considered better cut off. "How much autonomy do I have in choosing my relationships?" is key today when building new relationships and deciding on the degree of intimacy.

Social media platforms, the main axis underlying Index Relationships, are fundamentally self-centered mediums when it comes to relationship management. You have the choice to follow anyone at any time, and to unfollow just as easily. More recently, functions that allow users to specify to whom and to what extent personal content is accessible has further facilitated relationship management. In this sense social media platforms are a form of "asynchronous communication" that amplifies the level of self-centeredness in each interaction. Typically, communication is classified into "synchronous" and "asynchronous" depending on the time it takes to receive a reply from the other party. For example, communication methods in which conversation is in real time, such as phone calls and Zoom meetings, are classified as "synchronous communication." On the other hand, communication with a time lag, such as e-mail, text messages, Instagram direct messages, Facebook messages, and commenting on a post, are considered "asynchronous communication." In other words, social media platforms allow users to decide whether they want (and when) to reply. Users are able to use the direct message function as a type of real-time messenger as needed, and they are equally able to delay their responses by letting the messages pile up in their inboxes. In this context, modern society has become more comfortable accepting the characteristics of asynchronous relationships within social media platforms.

Outlook and Implications

People generally have stereotypes about what a good relationship entails. There is a preconception that it is better to be in a close relationship with a handful of people you can trust instead of having a wider network of shallow relationships. The notion is that close interactions with friends in the real world contribute to overall happiness significantly more than interactions with a group of random people met online. Of course, this notion cannot be ruled out. A 2015 Harvard University study conducted by the director of the Harvard Study of Adult Development, Robert Waldinger, found that relationships with high levels of intimacy and trust had a greater effect on happiness than those focused on building relationships solely with a large number of people. The longitudinal study, which began in 1938, involved 724 men over its 79-year run, with annual follow-ups of each subject.

Index Relationships from a business perspective

However, it is equally necessary to accept that a new way of forming relationships, one that did not exist before, also contributes to people's happiness in its own unique way. According to *The Strength of Weak Ties* by American sociologist Mark Granovetter, personal relationships are split between strong connections made with a few people and loose connections with a large number of people. Surprisingly, it was the loose connections that provided more of the quality information necessary for people's everyday lives, such as job opportunities. It makes sense that limiting interaction to a handful of close people may limit opportunities to acquire new information, given the group's comparable living environments and overlapping information. During a time of frequent relocations to new countries, had there been no new option to build relationships through Index Relationships, the loneliness that people felt would have been much greater.

In the future, companies should utilize Index Relationships to further their business operations. First, an "establish Index Relationships" function can be applied to a wide range of products and services. When designing products and services, this function should be considered at the very early stages of planning. LG U$^+$'s media content platform "U$^+$ Professional Baseball," for example, introduced a new chat function starting from the 2021 KBO season. Viewers can chat in private chat rooms while watching the broadcast for a more social experience. Watcha, an OTT service, has also introduced the "Watcha Party" feature on TV and mobile platforms in February 2022, where up to 2,000 people simultaneously access and chat in real time while watching the same show. Within three weeks of Watcha Party's mobile beta service launch, the cumulative number of parties reached 549,570, or a daily average of 3,870. The total number of messages hit 66,931,380 messages, or an average of 470,348 messages per day.

In December 2021, productivity platform Notion, which integrates and manages online work features such as notepads, documents, projects, and databases, launched a "résumé blind date" feature using its file sharing function. If users write and upload their résumé using the Notion tool, they can receive up to two other people's résumés for free every week and can chat with other users; making a résumé becomes a relationship-building tool. In other cases, these functions can also be applied to products. In August 2022,

Samsung Electronics announced that it would add the "Samsung Live Chat" function to smart TVs released after 2020. The service supports real-time chatting among viewers currently watching the same TV program. Once a chat room is opened for a specific drama or sports game, viewers can communicate with each other by sending messages via TV remote control or smartphone.

The characteristics of Index Relationship management can equally be applied in the organizational management setting of corporations. In an Index Relationship, the choice of whether to communicate or not lies with each individual. Feeling anxious about being unable to answer a call from the manager does not jive with today's workplace. It makes more sense to check messages left by the manager and follow up at a convenient time. This shift is also reflected in communication methods within the organization. The "Clips" feature in corporate messenger service Slack creates a short, recorded video clip that can be sent to the other party. This feature makes attending meetings optional. Rather than scheduling a meeting and gathering people at a set time, providing status updates and receiving reports when convenient for each party becomes an easy alternative.

• • •

Robin Dunbar claimed that no matter how socially

active a person is, the maximum number of stable relationships that a person can comfortably maintain is roughly 150 people. This number has been called "Dunbar's number." There are two main reasons behind the derivation of Dunbar's number. The first is cognitive limitation. Considering the size of a human cerebral cortex, which is responsible for information processing, the number of relationships that humans can remember and handle is 150 people. The second reason is time constraints. Time resources are finite. Expanding networks indefinitely is difficult due to the necessary choices about with whom and how to spend time. Will Dunbar's argument still be valid amid the surge of new social networking platforms? Aren't people already using the new mediums within finite resources to expand their relationships more efficiently?

Personal relationships, which are one of the most important aspects of a human life, are facing an unprecedented change. Now, the question is, in a society where these various indexes and methods of classification crisscross between us, how can we build happier relationships?

Irresistible!

The
'New Demand
Strategy'

How is new demand created? It is a crucial question all businesses must answer. Finding an answer to the question becomes even more pressing during times like now, when customers become reluctant to spend as they are faced with a recession, as well as during an age when a glut of similar products floods the markets. However, regardless of how many products are pouring out each day or how bad the economy is, consumers continue to be attracted to new experiences and are still happy to spend on novelties. In *Consumer Trend Insights 2023*, the strategy for creating a type of demand that can create an irresistible draw even amid market situations in which products and services are continuously being upgraded will be called the "New Demand" strategy. This refers to a methodology in which companies can create New Demand by developing irreplaceable products that consumers will have no choice but to buy.

The New Demand strategy classifies demand from the consumer side into two categories: "Replacement Demand," in which a consumer replaces a product that they are already using, and "New Demand," which encourages consumers to purchase a product that they do not currently own. Replacement Demand can be created by (1) upgrading; (2) adding a new design concept; and (3) changing payment methods. New Demand can be created by (1) offering products that have not existed before; (2) creating a new category of products; and (3) creating new products based on micro-segmentation. Creative thinking is crucial to developing new products that will attract consumers. To come up with something new one must deliberately think outside the box, try out foreign and outlandish concepts, dig deep into the product, and completely change consumers' mindsets. However, no matter how much creativity and advanced technology is applied to a product, it is difficult to succeed in the market if strategies are not devised from a consumer-oriented perspective. The answer must always come from the side of the customer.

How is new demand created? It is a crucial question for any business. In particular, the question is even more pressing during times like these, when customers become reluctant to spend as they face a recession, as well as during an age when a glut of similar products floods the markets. However, regardless of how many products are pouring out or how bad the economy is, consumers are attracted to new experiences and are happy to spend on novelties. When it comes to innovative products or services, even when there is no clear need for it at the moment and even when consumers need to cut down on spending, consumers ignore budget limitations and instead seek a reason to buy the new product. Creating such irresistible demand is the crucial strategy companies must master at this time.

In *Consumer Trend Insights 2023*, the strategy for creating demand for new products even in a market in which existing products and services are continuously upgraded will be called the "New Demand" strategy. In other words, it refers to a methodology that can create New Demand by developing irreplaceable products that consumers have no choice but to buy. In order for something to become an irreplaceable product, it must be completely different from alternatives. The rules of the game must be rewritten. New Demand describes that strategy. People say that opening someone else's wallet is one of the most difficult challenges in the world. When do consumers decide to spend? What kind of product does it take for them to say, "I'll buy it"?

From the consumer's point of view, demand can be divided into (1) a case of replacing a product that they already use and (2) the act of purchasing a new product that they do not currently own. The former is called "Replacement Demand" and the latter "New Demand." The following table summarizes the ways these demands are created.

New Demand is not a completely new concept, but rather a summary of existing methodologies. It is now being identified as a keyword because it is a topic that must be covered in detail considering its relevance to the business environment of 2023. During times of a "Disappearing Average" causing ordinary products to be overlooked, and when consumers are turning into "Cherry-sumers" as they enter ultra-saving mode, products that do not undergo the process of radical change and do not stand out on the shelf can no longer produce results for sellers. Given this change, we will offer a checklist for companies that are looking for ways of developing new products and fresh business models to follow. Let's examine the different types of New Demand

〈 Background and Method of Consumer Demand 〉

	Background	Method
Replacement Demand	**When you want to change the product you are using**	① Upgrade: When the product you use is better than the one you currently use - Upgrade of function and form factor - Continuous upgrade
		② Concept overlay: when new meaning is added to the product being used - Environmental concept - Premium concept
		③ Changing payment methods: when the psychological barrier to high prices is lowered - Installments, rentals, subscriptions, deferred payments (buy now, pay later[BNPL]), trade-ins
New Demand	**When you buy a new product you don't have**	① A "never seen before" product: a product that forms an ecosystem through disruptive innovation
		② Products that create a new category: products that fall outside existing categories
		③ Micro-segmentation of products: fine-tuned and particular purpose-driven products just for you - Consumer-based - Context-based

creation strategies that have been successful so far and see what companies can do with their existing capabilities.

Creation of Replacement Demand

It has been an ongoing challenge for managers to get consumers to make the decision to replace a product with a new model, especially if there is no problem with the product they are currently using. This process of creating deliberate obsolescence of a product for the purpose of increasing Replacement Demand for consumer goods is called "planned obsolescence." French philosopher Serge Latouche addresses this challenge in his book *Bon pour la casse: Les déraisons de l'obsolescence programmée (Good for Scrap: The Unreasonableness of Planned Obsolescence)*. Take the light bulb for example. Edison's first light bulb had a lifespan of 1,500 hours in 1881. That increased to 2,500 hours in the 1920s but is now only 1,000 hours. This encourages more frequent repeat purchases. Obsolescence includes "technical obsolescence," which adds new technology to new models to make existing products seem relatively outdated, and "psychological obsolescence," which gets people to desire new things beyond what they have. Latouche criticizes the environmental problems that arise from the wasted resources and the overflow of garbage caused by continuous creation of Replacement Demand through obsolescence.

Latouche's diagnosis makes sense. Even more so, with the development of social media, consumers have access to much more information than before which makes such tactics as deliberately shortening the lifespan of light bulbs risky. That could backfire and open companies up to become the target of criticism and boycotts from consumers. The creation of Replacement Demand by technological improvement which includes functions that customers need is the end goal for companies and is also beneficial to the lives of consumers. How do we create Replacement Demand that benefits both companies and customers? The answer can be broadly divided into three categories. First, "upgrade" a product to improve its function and appearance. Second, "overlay a fresh concept" to an existing product by adding a new design concept or angle. Third, "change the payment method" to make prices more acceptable.

1. Upgrade

Customers will be more than happy to pay up for a product if its features are significantly better than what they currently use. If a new computer gets faster, the monitor gets bigger, or your TV gets higher definition, people will be tempted to upgrade. This type of improvement of a product's specs includes both improvement of its functions and changes in its design or form factor. Let's take a deeper look at these cases.

1) Upgrade of function and form factor

Every new product release is marketed by emphasizing the improvements over its predecessor. However, whether that improvement is perceived as attractive enough to induce customers to make the purchase is another matter. In order for functional improvement to lead to Replacement Demand, a "unique selling proposition" (USP) for the product over its competitors is key. For example, the first generation of smartwatches focused on performing various functions when linked with a smartphone, mainly acting as a watch. The later-released Galaxy Watch and Apple Watch series emphasized health and safety functions that measure ECG and blood pressure and also make calls to preselected contacts in case of an emergency. Even for those who already own a smartwatch, these products and functions are an appealing proposition. Winia's electric rice cooker "Dimchae Cook" has a USP that is a level ahead from the existing competition, which has until now mostly focused on how well it can cook rice and other dishes. The added edge comes from successfully targeting health-conscious consumers and diabetics by offering a carbohydrate reduction function that cuts down the carbohydrates in cooked rice by up to 51%.

When companies offer a USP that consumers find attractive, even a small change to an existing product can make a significant contribution to increasing consumer demand. Improvement in the design of a product is one such upgrade. The external shape and physical specifications of a product are referred to as its "form factor," and design changes are typically made within this framework. Consumers typically have fixed stereotypes about a product's form factor. For example, since Steve Jobs first introduced the iPhone, smartphones have always been vertically longer and flat. Numerous improvements have been made to smartphones since then, but they have more or less all remained within the same form factor. Samsung Electronics, which faces stiff competition from Apple in the global smartphone market, has turned the tables by changing its form factor. With the launches of the Galaxy Z Flip and Z Fold it introduced a "folding" form factor, which created a new level of competition. Another example is the bladeless fan. Fans have long had the familiar design of spinning blades around a rotor. Dyson dramatically changed this form factor and introduced the bladeless fan, which enticed customers into buying the new product despite the relatively higher price. Innovative change in form factor results in strong Replacement Demand.

2) Continuous upgrades

At the time of writing, the iOS version of the iPhone operating system is 16.1. That means there have been 16 major improvements and many small tweaks in between. Continuous improvement is made in the field of software, which is where the term "upgrade" is most used. Upgraded hardware as well as software are released every year. The model names of popular smartphones released at the end of 2022 from Apple and Samsung are the iPhone 14 and Galaxy S22, respectively. The numbers suggest there has been a steady stream of upgrades over a long period of time. Such incremental innovation has its roots in the automotive industry.

Brands release a new model each year by improving upon the design or performance, and the changes are denoted with terms such as "full model change," "minor change," "face lift," or "model year change" depending on how extensive the changes have been. In the past, the cycle of a full model change in which the platform and engine of a car was upgraded had been about 5-7 years; but now as customer needs are diversifying and the speed of technological improvement is accelerating, the cycle is getting shorter. Now, the convenience offered from a car's features depends more on when it was released rather than on how luxurious it is.

New technology that offers a way for these upgrades to be made continuously to existing products is the latest development. By using "over-the-air (OTA)" technology, it is possible to update a vehicle's software by wirelessly modifying, adding, and deleting previous versions. It is possible to update the function without having to bring the car to the service center. OTA is becoming increasingly important not only because of how convenient it is to have software defects related to vehicle operation fixed, or to have navigation maps updated. It's also important to maintain the autonomous driving function by sending and receiving signals between vehicles on the road, which requires constant OTA updates. In addition, accumulating big data on driving conditions is essential for product improvement or improving maintenance in the future. As a car's autonomous driving function becomes more important, these cars are now recognized as "electronic products" and even "communication devices" rather than "machinery."

A similar concept is being applied to electronic products in general. LG Electronics launched a series of upgradable home appliances in January 2022 which will have their software upgraded continuously, much like Tesla's automotive software. The more users use their home appliances, the more the relevant functions are updated through LG's smart home platform "ThinQ." In addition, the home appliances feature new functions such as the ability to download new UI, sound, and graphic interfaces at any time. LG introduced what it calls the "MoodUP" refrigerator as part of its upgradeable home appliances lineup at the IFA trade show, Europe's largest consumer electronics show, held in Berlin, Germany in September 2022. The MoodUP refrigerator uses special panels with LEDs that connect to the ThinQ app and allow the user to change the colors of the four upper and lower refrigerator door panels. This has attracted the attention of the younger generations who are interested in home interior design. The MoodUP refrigerator, which can also play music according to the time of day, shows the added value these functions of upgradeable home appliances provide.

Continuous upgrades present a dilemma from the company's point of view. This is because incentives for consumers to purchase a new version of their products will increase if upgrades are not available for their existing products. If the operating system of existing mobile phones can be upgraded so the functions of the new product can be used with the old device, there is little reason to purchase a new product. So why do companies continue to offer upgrades? This is because the smartphone is an important part of the wider ecosystem of a company's full range of products and services. Smartphones are not simply devices that exist on their own but have wider applications in other sectors such as the app market. The types of apps used vary depending on whether the user is using an iPhone with iOS or a Samsung with Android. Therefore, there is an incentive to "lock-in" customers by providing continuous upgrades. As described above, the reason that cars and home appliances recently started offering upgradable services reflects the emergence of an ecosystem for these industries in which connectivity among these products grows.

2. Overlaying a new concept

Even if the product itself does not change, if its perception changes, it can be considered something new. We will call the method of making consumers aware of a new angle by promoting conceptual change rather than changes of the product's functional properties "concept overlay컨셉 덧입히기."

1) Environmental concept

The concept that consumers want from a product often changes with the times. A retro feel, a deliberately tacky design, or a store that helps neighbors in need are some examples of concepts that have attracted consumers and for which demand has changed over time. The hottest topic these days is the environment. With the emergence and awareness of ESG (environmental, social, and corporate governance), the 'E', environmental, has garnered fervid attention as a hot concept. Many companies are working on adding value through catering to this trend.

Volvo Group has introduced a cyclical business model which aims to make every car part available for reuse through Volvo itself or its suppliers. To this end, it announced plans to drastically change the existing design, development, and manufacturing environment of its cars. Volvo remanufactured about 40,000 parts starting in 2021, achieving a remarkable feat of reducing carbon dioxide emissions by about 3,000 tons and recycling about 95%

of production waste. Furthermore, it is setting its sights on recycling electric vehicle batteries. LG Electronics is also moving toward recycling used materials by using recycled plastics extracted from used home appliances. The newly launched furniture-style air purifier "Aero Furniture," targeting Generation MZ, has utilized recycled plastic materials. It is made in the shape of a table with customizable tabletops, such as a limited-edition dodo bird version. The dodo bird is known as a representative species of extinction.

2) Premium concept

The high-end market is always in good shape regardless of how well the economy is doing. A consumer's desire to have a coveted item is unaffected by broader market forces. Moreover, among these products, prominent brands have come to play the role of status symbols. The luxury goods market has been getting bigger as people show off their spending through social media.

Even within the high-end market, the concepts of "premium" and "luxury" are slightly different. "Luxury" usually refers to a brand that has deep roots in history and tradition. Due to the heritage of the brand, even if another company produces the same product with much higher quality, it cannot easily overtake the luxury brand's status. Well-known luxury brands such as Hermès, Louis Vuitton, and Chanel fall into this category. On the other hand, "premium" refers to a broader spectrum in which companies that make mass products also make high-quality products that are produced by adding a layer of technology and quality. A good example is Toyota Motor Corporation and its premium brand Lexus which has been in production for over 30 years alongside Toyota's production of mid- to low-priced mass cars.

The strategy that Korean companies should pursue is not a "luxury" strategy but a "premium" strategy. When a product successfully takes on a premium concept, it can spur new demand in the luxury sector. A prime example is Hyundai Motor's Genesis brand. In Hyundai's product segmentation, which ranged in order from high to low, Equus, Genesis, Grandeur ("Azera" in the North American market), Sonata, and Avante ("Elantra" in many international markets), it succeeded in spinning off Genesis as a new and independent premium brand. A comparable example in the home appliance market is LG Electronics' "Signature" series. With the concept of "work in life," Signature successfully established its brand image of recognizing and celebrating the value of repetitive and boring daily chores. It is a successful example of combining modern design and sophisticated brand marketing.

3. Changing payment methods:
rentals, subscriptions, post-payments

Even if there is no change in the function or concept of a product, Replacement Demand can still be created if the cost burden of buying the product is reduced. In addition to traditional installment payments and rental plans, there are also subscription plans currently available in various industries, BNPL (buy now, pay later), and trade-ins as different forms of payment.

One of the most common reasons for people not being able to buy something they want is that it is too expensive. One way to still get the item is to split up the payment. Paying in installments has a long history. Rentals are also a reinterpretation of the traditional installment concept. When paying in installments, ownership passes to the buyer and the amount to pay is spread out over a set number of months, whereas a rental literally means borrowing the item while paying a usage fee. There is an added incentive to get a product as a rental because although the product is not owned, it can be used as if it were one's own for a certain period of time, all while the economic burden on the consumer is reduced.

Coway is a brand that has achieved great success by offering rentals for home appliances, a big change from rentals previously which had been mainly used for automobiles. Chairman Yoon Seok-geum, who is known as a master of sales, entered the water purifier business in 1989 by establishing Coway Korea, the predecessor of Coway. Eight years later, he faced financial challenges due to the 1997 Asian financial crisis. There were hardly any consumers who would buy a water purifier, which was priced at 1 million won per unit at the time – a hefty price during an economic crisis. Chairman Yoon said, "If it won't sell anyway, why not lend it out?" With that in mind, the idea of renting a home appliance was born. By attracting consumers who had been reluctant to purchase an expensive water purifier, the company was able to sell 100,000 rental water purifiers within one year of its launch. It is a classic and well-known method, and it still applies to the market in 2023, where customers' purchasing power is expected to decline along with the economic downturn.

Recently, "subscription" has become an even hotter keyword than "rental." A subscription is a payment method in which a product is delivered periodically as consumers pay a certain amount every month, as in the case of a newspaper or a magazine. In most cases, the contract is repeated without an end date. Customers do not have to worry about paying for each individual item, and companies can expect a fixed and stable income stream, so the target industry of the subscription business model is expanding.

According to the Korea Consumer Agency, subscriptions can be classified into several categories depending on whether the target product is accessible online or is a physical product, and whether the consumer personally chooses each item or receives a curated product. The types of subscriptions include (1) licensing subscriptions, such as usage of software or a cloud service; (2) curation subscriptions, where new products arrive regularly, such as cosmetics and traditional liquor; and (3) delivery subscriptions, where the same products arrive regularly, such as razors or diapers.

Credit cards have long eased the burden of big-ticket purchases and tempted consumers to spend more. However, as online transactions became common in the United States in 2021, a deferred payment model called "buy now, pay later (BNPL)" was introduced and caught on rapidly. BNPL was introduced in every major American brand's online store, such as GAP, Adidas, Sephora, and H&M. Instead of the consumer, a payment company first pays the full price of the product to the merchant and the consumer then pays the product price to the payment company over several installments every two weeks.

It resembles installment payments using a credit card, but the difference is that anyone over the age of 18 is able to use the service immediately by downloading a BNPL app (such as Affirm or Afterpay) and signing up for the service. Criteria such as credit ratings when applying for a credit card are not required. There is no installment interest or fees that vary depending on a person's credit rating, so it has soared in popularity among American millennials who have many things that they want to buy but lack consistent incomes. The business model has been hit by the high delinquency rate of customers and the issue of regulating the market amid a separate set of regulations being applied to big tech companies issuing BNPL services on top of existing credit card companies is yet to be resolved. But the launch of Apple Pay Later is a sign that reflects the lasting growth potential of the industry.

Sometimes the reason that people don't replace a product is because they already own a working version. Here, the way to generate Replacement Demand is to encourage people to discard the old product. These "trade-ins" mainly occur in the furniture and electronics industries, where the product replacement cycle is long. IKEA offers a "buyback service" to repurchase its own products, while home furnishing company Casamia offers exchanges with discounts of up to 30% when replacing products in the same category. Global electronics companies such as Dyson and Apple also offer trade-in services.

Creating New Demand

Companies get business by convincing people to replace their existing products with new ones, but a more fundamental demand creation strategy is to develop a completely new product that has never existed before. It cannot be overestimated just how much New Demand has arisen across various sectors after the release of the smartphone. Creating New Demand through the development of completely new products is the dream of every business and is at the core of product planning. This is because such breakthroughs are a result of the perfect alignment of technological achievements and understanding consumer tastes. This is a very difficult task, but the rewards of success are unparalleled.

Indeed, not every company can create a product as revolutionary as the smartphone. Even if it is possible, it is not something that can be done often. However, it is possible to launch new innovative products that are within a range of existing products. A new hit product is born when it can save consumers' time and reduce their effort, or when it gives customers a new awareness for an existing product that is entertaining. A typical way to do this is by leveraging existing technology to create a new category of products, or by focusing on a small but distinct customer segment.

1. "Never seen before" demand

Clayton Christensen, an academic, business consultant, and professor at Harvard Business School, divides technological innovation into "sustaining innovation" and "disruptive innovation." When it comes to performance-enhancing technology, sustaining innovation is a technology that can generate Replacement Demand by improving the performance of existing products, while disruptive innovation is a technology that attracts a new group of customers by introducing a different value proposition in a completely different area, even if the technology offered is at a lower level than what the existing customers require. In the end, disruptive innovation creates unprecedented demand by offering products that are cheaper, simpler, smaller, and more convenient to use than existing products.

As shown in the table, the products Christensen identifies as disruptive technology are those that go beyond the existing paradigm. Disruptive innovations are so-called "game changers" that are different from the products and services that currently exist. In order to create a new product based on disruptive technology, a long preparation process is required in which an entire ecosystem that supports the new product's innovative technology is created along with the product itself.

Take the electric vehicle for example. It was 1990, more than 30 years ago, when General Motors (GM) unveiled the world's first electric vehicle to be mass produced from 1996 to 1999: the EV1. However, despite widespread expectation that electric cars would revolutionize the automobile industry and dramatically contribute to a cleaner environment, the EV1 was completely scrapped in 2003, with existing

⟨ Comparison of Existing Technologies and Disruptive Technologies ⟩

Existing technology	Disruptive technology
Traditional photo	Digital photo
Telephone	Wireless telephone
Laptop computer	Mobile device
Desktop computer	PlayStation

Source: Christensen [1997], *The Innovator's Dilemma*

cars being recalled and destroyed and a small number being donated to some museums and academic institutions. There was much talk about the failure that even a documentary, *Who Killed the Electric Car?*, was released. Some criticized GM's irresponsibility for getting rid of EV1s just after they met the California Air Resources Board's mandate to produce a certain quota of zero-emissions vehicles, while others blamed the lobbying of large oil companies who wanted to keep internal combustion engine vehicles on the road. Disruptive innovation can only have a lasting foothold in the market when an infrastructure or ecosystem – charging stations in the case of electric vehicles – is built, alongside with consumer awareness, and government regulations and support. From that standpoint, the rapid increase in the number of electric vehicles in recent years can be seen as the fact that the ecosystem has only now been effectively put together.

2. Products that create new markets

As previously mentioned, it is not easy to develop a completely new product based on disruptive innovation. However, by tweaking existing technologies and concepts, new categories of products and markets can be created. For example, Winia's Dimchae is a successful case of this method in which Winia changed its category of products that did not sell, in this case repurposing small refrigerators to be marketed as being specialized for kimchi. As the number of single-person households and families increases and people eat less kimchi, that category has been adapted to include specialized products for dry aging meat, as well as for storage for salad and baby food ingredients.

A new category of products that drew attention at IFA 2022 was LG Electronics' new home appliance that stores and displays shoes called "ShoeCase." Some might ask, "who needs to exhibit their shoes?" But for avid shoe collectors who stay up all night to get a pair of limited-edition sneakers, this is a completely different story. Among millennial collectors who treasure their collections of favorite sneakers, these sneakers are regarded as an example of the "Digging Momentum" trend. The shoe display case is a new category of home appliances that targets these consumers. It maintains the most appropriate temperature and humidity to keep the shoes in top condition as one would store an art collection in a museum, and it also provides an appealing visual display that rotates 360 degrees, illuminated with hip lighting. Whether this new category of appliances made for shoe care and display will be able to follow in the footsteps of LG's "Styler" steam closets is yet to be seen.

Even though technology among existing kitchen appliances is largely constrained by what is already out there, some new concepts have managed to emerge. One example is Samsung Electronics' "Bespoke Cuker": a kitchen appliance that is an all-in-one grill, air fryer, microwave, and toaster. Through collaboration with Samsung Card, they have added the convenience of the subscription model to home appliances. If a user signs up for the "Cuker Plan," they can receive a new oven for 50,000 won and spend the monthly fee at the online "e-food hall" dedicated to Cuker. In this food hall, 18 food specialty brands such as CJ Cheil-Jedang, Ottogi, Pulmuone, and Dongwon offer their products which are easily compatible with Cuker's functions. Starting with Cuker, Samsung Electronics is kicking off the subscription model for its products, essentially turning its products into a subscription service. Notably, this example encompasses multiple New Demand creation strategies including the convergence of existing technologies into new products, payment plans, and curation of products to be used in conjunction with one another.

3. Micro-segmentation products

The "Bradley Timepiece" is a watch for the visually impaired. Users can check the time by touching two marbles and a ticker hand that moves along the surface. Considering the proportion of visually impaired people among the total population, this watch was aimed at a narrow market, yet it was very popular with the general public as well. This is because users are able to check the time when it is difficult to do so, such as in a dark theater or during a meeting. Furthermore, the aesthetics and unique design along with the symbolism of working with the visually impaired brought greater awareness and contributed to the watch's popularity. Its success has significant implications because it shows that even a product targeting a very narrow market can end up as a competitive product in the broader market.

Focusing on the needs of a very specific target market and making consumers feel that a product is made with them in mind is called "micro-segmentation." "Segmentation" originally meant classifying consumers according to certain criteria to help businesses with their marketing goals. In the past, the main task was to identify the largest average mass market in order to generate maximum sales. Micro-segmentation can either be based on a consumer type or a specific context.

Japanese towel maker The Towel makes separate towels for men and women. When using a towel, women tend to dab their skin with the towel, while men use broader strokes. Considering this difference, The Towel segmented men's and women's towels by varying the softness of the thread material and the number of times the filaments are spun. Along these lines, Aveda's combs are divided into pre-shampoo and post-shampoo types. Before shampooing, users can use the "Scalp Brush" to clean their scalp when it is dry, and then use the "Wooden Paddle Brush" after shampooing to restore smoothness and shine to the hair. The aforementioned Bradley Timepieces and towels for men and women generate New Demand through micro-segmentation with the consumer in mind.

Then there are cases where products are specialized and developed for different contexts. A prime example can be found in the gaming sector where a variety of products tailored to the needs of gamers are being introduced. Samsung Electronics introduced the 4K gaming monitor "Odyssey Ark," which offers a 55-inch curved display that can be divided into three sections, rotatable horizontally and vertically according to the game, providing an immersive experience. In addition to the realistic feeling of sitting in a spaceship, it also has a vertical cockpit mode and an innovative interface that allows the user to adjust the screen to the desired size and ratio.

There are also changes taking place in the automobile market, where choosing and purchasing from a handful of premade vehicles had been the standard way to go. Until recently, cars have always been classified by the "segment" concept which divides cars into categories based on their size. But now, segmentation is being subdivided further along the purpose-based vehicle (PBV) concept which looks at a car's purpose for use. PBV includes delivery vehicles such as refrigerated trucks, specialized vehicles for car-hailing services such as Uber, leisure vehicles such as camping vehicles, and vehicles for the disabled. PBVs are multi-purpose mobility vehicles that are made according to a business's purposes and a customer's needs. In the past, after purchasing a light commercial vehicle (such as the Hyundai Starex or Volkswagen Transporter), customers had to remodel it themselves to meet their own needs. But PBV is a new business model that can produce customized vehicles with the customer's special purpose in mind from the early development stages. Kia Corporation has held a conference with potential partners such as Uber and Coupang in September 2022 and is playing a leading role in the development of PBVs that can provide solutions tailored to customer needs from the initial stages of vehicle planning.

The reason for targeting a niche market rather than a large mass market is clear. This is because, in order to secure sales with limited resources in a situation where market competition is growing and the economy is declining, the "purchase conversion rate" has become more important than just raising brand awareness or improving favorable attitudes. In other words, it is more effective to increase purchase conversion by focusing on a small number of customers in a market and meeting their needs.

Outlook and Implications

How can we create new growth in an uncertain market environment?

This is a question that has not changed throughout the history of economics. The reason why this question, which is not a trend in itself, was discussed in detail is because of the challenging business environment expected in 2023. During a time when an unprecedented recession is expected, consumers such as "Cherry-sumers" are cutting down on spending, and even the prevailing stereotypes of the "Average" are disappeearing. While explaining the New Demand creation methodology and New Demand strategy, this book does not approach the problem from the supply side or use TRIZ (the Soviet-era acronym for "theory of inventive problem solving": a methodological approach utilized in various industries). Rather, we ask: "When does a *consumer* replace and purchase a product?" All questions in modern management must start from the consumer.

Humans instinctively seek efficiency. This will increasingly be the case among companies and organizational management which require maximum output while controlling input. Therefore, in the field of product development, companies tend to want to achieve maximum performance by making minimum changes. But long term, this is not a good strategy. If companies benchmark successful products and release slightly modified and improved products, they may succeed in minimizing costs and risks; but in a market where consumer information is transparent, the company's image may be stigmatized for selling a "copied product" or being a "lazy company." The bigger, more serious problem is the fact that as companies get used to following trends, the value of the company will slowly suffer.

Creative thinking is required to come up with a new product that can attract consumers. Companies have to intentionally deviate from the norm, make new attempts as much as possible, dig deep into consumer tastes, and be armed with a fresh and open mindset. In order to do that, companies must redefine their technology and offer consumers the excitement of the unexpected. Yet even then, if this creative thinking process is not based on a consumer-oriented point of view, it is difficult to succeed in the market. Sony's Betamax video format, which featured advanced technology at the time but still failed to create demand and set a new standard in the market, or 3D TV, which despite huge marketing efforts did not survive because consumers were uncomfortable wearing special glasses, are representative examples. The words of Masuda Muneaki, the founder of Tsutaya Books in Japan and author of *Theory of Intellectual Capital*, are apt:

"The solution always comes from the customer. Answers from sources other than the customer are ultimately self-righteous."

디깅모멘텀

The number of people who are getting serious about their hobbies is on the rise. Although the subject of their focus is rather narrow and the degree of immersion is quite deep, they are not trying to escape reality. Instead, these people actively choose to invest their time, money, and energy in their hobby of choice, and through that are enthusiastic about life. We would like to call this trend of people digging deeply into a specific interest or hobby "Digging Momentum." Digging Momentum isn't just a hobby, though – it is an active process in which people are trying to find their true selves in the "multi-persona" era, and it is a struggle to actively find where one's source of happiness lies to help cope with existential anxiety caused by the pandemic and recession.

Followers of this "digging" activity can be divided into three types. The "concept type" who focus on a specific idea or image in order to find entertainment value or add motivation to daily life; the "relational type" who like the same topic and join others to further dive into a subject through active communication; and the "collecting type" who enjoy showing off through racking up several topics and interests they are passionate about. As more people get serious about their own niche interests, related industries such as entertainment, content creators, and purveyors of "kidult" (kid+adult) toys are also growing. Furthermore, the rising influence of these "diggers" means their role in marketing efforts in various industries is becoming more important.

It is difficult to draw a precise line between what type of digging constitutes an escape from reality and what is simply a deeper look into the self, but it is necessary to be able to find the right balance in daily life when digging. The key is growth. When the activity can be harmonized with daily life under the broader direction of self-improvement, digging can become momentum for real progress in people's lives.

*S*cene #1 *I am Hermione, the pretty girl from House Gryffindor*

I am Hermione. I love to study. Since I am British, I have to be particularly good at English, my native language. The top score in the class for this exam is of course going to me, but in order to beat my competitor, Malfoy, I have to study hard and not let my guard down.

This type of "concept study method" has become a popular trend among some students. As in the example above, the concept "Hermione, the pretty girl from House Gryffindor in the 'Harry Potter' series" is selected, then used as a way to provide motivation to improve grades in certain subjects. The concept is more than just a mental image – items such as a Harry Potter notebook, a Gryffindor scarf, a Hermione headband, and a magic wand are used. Even a YouTube video of Gryffindor-themed ASMR can be used to complete the concept. These props, such as "Hogwarts Admission Sets" and "House Gryffindor Sets," can actually be found on sale from online bookstores.

Scene #2   An idol fan in their 30s

I still like idols. It isn't long before I hit my 40s, but when it comes to liking idols, my age is just a number. I first liked idols in my early teens, so it is not a stretch to say that 70% of my life was consumed by idols. How many idols have I watched enlist in the army? If the age gap between me and the younger idol was five years or less, I called them "oppa." If they were good looking, then he was my oppa. But at an age difference of about ten years, I suddenly feel like a mother figure...

The age range of idol fans is broadening. Many idol fans say they never imagined they would be like this at their current age as the title of a local book on fandom suggests. The book starts out by saying when other people are watching romance dramas, idol fans are preoccupied watching the performance of their favorite star, and when other people buy clothes and go on a trip, these fans buy idol star-branded merchandise. They download the picture of their favorite member in a split second, change their phone's wallpaper to their favorite pop group member, purchase unnecessary cosmetics or game items just to win the chance to see their idol, and make trips to the subway station or restaurant that their favorite member was last seen in.

Scene #3   Lego fans invited to the Lego headquarters

Everyone who plays with Legos has a dream of becoming a Lego designer. I never thought that could become a reality; but I got a call from the headquarters setting up an interview with me. It was a first for someone in Korea. Everything felt like a dream — it was great.

Architectural designer Lee Jae-won (36) was invited to the Lego headquarters in Denmark for an interview after a Lego project he had made in his spare time and posted on Facebook went viral. Game company developer Park Chi-hoon (41) is also a Lego fanatic. Since Lego's Star Wars series was released in 1999, his collection now fills an entire room. The age of "Legomaniacs," or those addicted to Lego, is growing. Lego is also becoming somewhat of a financial investment. As the number of Lego fanatics grows, more people are looking to buy discontinued, rare models, that fetch a high price in the second-hand market. *The Telegraph,* after comparing the growth rate of used prices of limited-edition Lego sets released over the past 15 years with the return on investment in gold and stocks, concluded that investing in Lego was much more profitable.

The Positive Side of Being Overly Engrossed: 'Digging'

What the previous three cases have in common is people

who are excessively engrossed in a certain activity. Whether it be a concept, a relationship, or a collection, the engrossing activity "digs" deeper than a mere hobby and has a different connotation. To people who are not interested in the activity or subject (whom the "diggers" refer to as "muggles"), diggers may seem strange and eccentric. But they do not care. Although the subject of their focus is rather narrow and the degree of immersion is quite deep, they are not trying to escape reality. Instead, these people actively choose to invest their time, money, and energy in their interest of choice, and through that are enthusiastic about life.

For *Consumer Trend Insights 2023,* we would like to name the trend of people digging deeply into a field that suits their taste "Digging Momentum." Although this phenomenon is sometimes derided as simply being overly preoccupied or obsessed with a certain topic, the negative connotation and perception these activities once had is gradually fading. We suggest "digging" to be a more neutral term that more closely describes the trend. The diggers that are spread throughout our society cannot be written off as being merely "too serious about their hobbies." Digging is an active process in which people are trying to find their true selves in the "multi-persona" era, and it is a struggle to find a source of happiness to help cope with existential anxiety caused by the pandemic and recession.

The word "digging" is being used in a different way in

Korea. In the field of pop music, the term was first used to describe the actions of musical artists who would search for new genres of music and analyze trends in popular music in depth. In a span of less than three years, this activity has expanded far enough into other sectors to be noticed as a trend, now referred to as "Digging Momentum." The act of being obsessed with one's favorite subject and pouring time and energy into it is not a new phenomenon. The Japanese term *"otaku"* is used to describe a person immersed in a specific subculture such as animation at a professional level, and the Korean word *"dukhoo*덕후*"* and the English words "geek" or "nerd" are also used to describe a person who is passionate about a certain subject but lacks social skills. There have been several groups of people who are overly enthralled by their areas of interest in the past, including those referred to as "Fansumers," a keyword from *Consumer Trend Insights 2020* for those who engage in aggressive and active fandom of celebrities, politicians, and brands. So how does "digging" differ from these past concepts?

First, as the digger's target topic of interest widens, as does the number of screens each person has access to, media content including dramas, movies, comics, and novels have become new categories of interests for diggers to become obsessed with. Watching programs and reruns across several platforms and then editing and cutting up scenes in 0.1-second increments to be shared as photos or short videos with other diggers creates connections. Moreover, their purpose of digging is not just personal entertainment. They like sharing their experiences and showing off because they have invested that much time and dedication. As a result, these diggers become influencers by taking control of how they consume media or products, rather than being led by the marketing strategies created by companies. Therefore, digging is a new concept in which the immersive behaviors defined in terms such as *"otaku,"* "geek/nerd," and "Fansumer" emerge in a new light, as leaders of mainstream opinion on social media.

The English word "momentum" is a word mainly used in Korea in regard to physics. In recent years, in politics and economics, it is used in the expanded sense to describe a catalyst in which the direction of stock prices turns. The fact that digging is not merely the extension of a hobby, but also a catalyst or a turning point to find one's true identity and happiness, is the reason why we would like to use the term "Digging Momentum."

Diggers can be divided into three types: the "conceptual type," the "relational type," and the "collection type." First, the conceptual type focuses on a specific concept for the sake of enjoying the feeling of being captivated by the subject. This includes applying a detailed theme to make daily life more interesting or using it as a way to enjoy media content. Second, the relational type delves further into a subject through active communication between people who share the same interest, and they are more interested in the process of sharing and communicating between people with similar tastes. Whether online or offline, they share common interests and enjoy working together in the process of learning more about their favorite topic. Third, the collection type seeks fulfillment through sharing or showing off their knowledgeable collection of multiple interests and experiences. Now, let's take a closer look at what kind of Digging Momentum is emerging for each of the three types, what is behind this trend, and what it means for society and different industries. Let's dig in!

Types and Aspects of 'Digging Momentum'

1. Conceptual Digging

"I used to act as if I was a student with top grades, but then I ended up making a hobby out of studying and made it to graduate school. Don't say acting out a conceptual image is awkward – if you start living life like that, life becomes more interesting……"

This is a post found on an online community. As a digger that dug into acting out the concept of "studious person," they ended up being accepted to graduate school. As mentioned in the introduction, this study method is popular among students these days. The types include the "princess concept," the "Hermione concept," and the "law school concept." Their immersion in these conceptual images begins with repeating the details of the concept in their minds. With retro and Y2K styles trending recently, the "American teenage movie concept" is another popular concept. A digger imagines herself to be the most popular girl in high school that has a crush on the smartest nerd in the school, so now she has a reason to study hard. To get in character, she puts her hair in a high ponytail, plays music from a playlist that has songs from teenage movies, and plays ambient sounds of a New York morning from ASMR clips on YouTube.

The whole process can come off as absurd to many people, but the key to immersion in this case is staying in character. By choosing and identifying with a conceptual image from a subject they are interested in, diggers are able to find more motivation and efficiency in performing tasks like studying, which otherwise may be difficult for them to concentrate on.

The concept here doesn't have to be as far-fetched as being a princess or the main character of a teen romance novel. Instead, it would be easier to act out a concept in a story so ordinary that all of us will have experienced it at least once. The latest trend that characterizes online dramas and comedy shows are hyper-realistic narratives. An example is the YouTube channel "Pickgo," which averages over 1 million views, even though it uses familiar storylines that are not special in any way. In Pickgo, clips with titles such as "Characteristics of people who have never had a social life," "Characteristics of overly serious people," and "Characteristics of people dating with low self-esteem" can be found. These clips are so realistic that they either remind people of themselves or their acquaintances, making it easy to act out in real life. The YouTube channel "Short Box," which reenacts everyday life in the form of a short comedy clip between one and ten minutes, also attracted 2.19 million subscribers in 2022 with its hyper-realistic content such as "Long-term relationships," "Brothers," and "Drunk conversations."

Acting out concepts is also popular on TikTok, the hottest platform among Generation Z. Posts with the #POV ("point of view") hashtag are popular. For example, users make a single video by connecting short videos that act out everyday situations such as "falling in love with your boyfriend," "breaking up with your boyfriend," and "meeting a new boyfriend." These videos combine acting skills, makeup, costumes, and props which are used to make the situation seem even more convincing, as if the viewer is talking directly to the person on the screen. This hashtag hit more than 600 billion views as of August 2022, and several TikTokkers have reenacted their own version of popular clips, giving viewers more options to choose from.

There are also many social media accounts that provide specialized information about a certain concept. Twitter, where the bot trend has been growing, is a typical example. A "bot" refers to an account that automatically tweets at certain times during the day like a robot. For example, if you follow a professional sports team bot, game information of that team will be updated regularly. However, recently the term also refers to a trend in which a human user pretends to be a robot and sends out messages like a bot. For example, the "Today's Random Knowledge Bot오늘의랜덤지식봇," which manually informs subscribers of random bits of knowledge, introducing more than 180 pieces of miscellaneous knowledge, has posted about things that people have probably never been curious about: for example "Japanese orthodontic surgery" and "hamsters' inability to get drunk," are uploaded along with cute illustrations, catching the interest of its followers which as of August 2022 have exceeded 380,000 followers.

There are restaurants that are gaining popularity by using a unique concept to cater to consumers immersed in a certain subject. Australian interactive restaurant Karen's Diner acts out the concept of being "the rudest place in the world." Employees ignore customers waiting to be served, play games on their mobile phones, or become annoyed by calls from customers trying to place an order. When a customer asks for more ketchup, they throw it at them. Customers are entertained by this and try to elicit ruder responses from the staff. The restaurant has become popular with concept-loving Generation MZ and has expanded to more than 11 branches globally, including in the US and UK. Being competitive in terms of taste and menu offerings is now the bare minimum. Diggers are fascinated by unique concepts that have never been seen before.

2. Relational Digging

The negative connotation of the term "*fanjil*팬질," which typically refers to the aggressive celebrity fandom of immature teenagers, is fading away. Instead, being an overenthusiastic fan has become an activity for any age group, and even a badge of honor. There are many elderly passionate fans in the fan clubs of BTS and singer Lim Young-woong. Declaring yourself a "*dukhoo*덕후" who is passionate about some celebrity is called "*duk*ming out," refering to "coming out" to the world about one's celebrity obsession. Though many *dukhoos* may have been hiding under the cover of online anonymity, the biggest advantage of *duk*ming out is that they can then find out how many other people share their tastes, and then share information and interests with the group of like-minded *dukhoos*. This type of communication among people with similar tastes, delving deeper into a topic or interest together, is called "relational digging."

The most common subjects of relational digging are singers, idols, actors, and cartoon characters, which are referred to as "*dukjoo*덕주." *Dukjoo* can be literally translated as "the *dukhoo's* master or owner." For example, if someone is into BTS, then that person is a *dukhoo* and BTS is the *dukjoo*. The process of getting to know more about the *dukjoo* is a form of relational digging in the sense that it does not end with a one-sided interest in a celebrity but grows *dukhoos'* knowledge and interest through communicating with other similarly minded *dukhoos*.

Relational digging starts off by following a set sequence. In order to become a "*dukchin*덕친(friend of a *dukhoo*)," *dukhoos* must first get to know one another's tastes. They might organize their favorite idols by year and upload them to a social media account or build rapport by sharing past experiences of falling out of love with certain idols – and sharing who their latest crush is. This personal history of supporting a certain celebrity is referred to as a "fan chronicle덕질연대기." In the process of getting to know one another's chronicles, the chances of finding a close match for someone to communicate with goes up. Generation MZ likes to classify personality and behavioral characteristics of both themselves or their friends using classifications such as an MBTI test to identify friends who fit or do not fit. This is similar to the method used in finding compatible diggers. Personality classification platform Poomang품맹 provides a fan personality test service that helps identify the type of digger the user is. Through this platform, users can identify similar types and find friends with whom they would work well together.

If people find a *dukchin* using this method, it is likely they also click in real life when they meet offline and become friends to enjoy a "*dukhoo tour*" together. A "*dukhoo tour*" is a tour where fans visit the restaurants and cafes of their favorite idol or go to a place where fans gather to share their love for their celebrity.

When a TV drama becomes a hit, secondary content called "fake dramas" also gain popularity. JTBC's YouTube channel "Drama Voyage" produced a completely new fake drama called *Strange First Love Song Ji-won* just by editing clips from old dramas in which actors Park Eun-bin and Kang Tae-oh appeared. These two were the lead actors of the hit drama series *Extraordinary Attorney Woo*이상한 변호사 우영우. Fans have praised the fake drama for having a storyline strong enough to be aired independently. CJ ENM's YouTube channel "Sharping" also produced a fake reality show called *EXchange Cells*환승세포 by re-editing the reality show *EXchange 2* 환승연애2 and popular drama *Yumi's Cells 2* 유미의 세포들 2. These new projects by broadcasters are meaningful in that they provide a forum for diggers who are obsessed with certain programs to gather and express their love for their favorite actors.

3. Collection Digging

One way to understand someone is to look into their room. In his book *Snoop: What Your Stuff Says About You*, Sam Gosling, a psychologist at the University of Texas at Austin, says that people put objects that reflect their tastes in the space they live to, consciously or unconsciously, express their identity. For example, some place stuffed animals around the bed for emotional support, or stack expensive luxury brand products on shelves to display their high tastes. These are ways a digger's room can showcase their "collection type" personality.

Recently, the hottest objects to collect have been "character toys." It is said that the happiness derived from looking at something cute is on par with the pleasure derived from food. That is why some people fill their surroundings with cute items. In May 2022, 7-Eleven released three types of toys called "My Character Keyrings캐릭터 마이키링" consisting of Pokémon, Crayon Shin-chan, and Sanrio characters. Cumulative sales exceeded 2 million units in just two months. Several specialized online platforms have been launched to facilitate trading of this kind of character merchandise. Thinggo띵고, the first so-called "fun-shop" that opened in Korea, is gaining popularity among pop culture fans interested in collecting and selling merchandise related to popular animation characters from the US, Europe, Japan, and China. It has received 2 billion won in funding from Stonebridge

Ventures and other investors. Colley, a taste sharing platform, operates its own shop based on character IPs (intellectual property) from Harry Potter, Crayon Shin-chan, and Disney. Since it is only possible to purchase certain toys under the Colley line through this website, the platform has become a favorite among the growing number of diggers who collect character products.

Collection digging is not just about collecting. Showing off is a necessary component. Rather than just waiting for likes by simply posting their collections on social media, they seek ways to make their collections look more interesting and to get more attention. A typical example is a recent trend on TikTok. Videos with the hashtag #collectorcheck on TikTok show off users' collections. Some of the clips might be titled "my most expensive item," "something everybody wants to have," "the first thing I bought," or "the strangest thing I own," which are posted using the soundtrack of the video uploaded by a TikTokker named Samantha in the background. The collection features a number of items, everything from the once popular Pop-it (a silicone toy version of bubble wrap) to Starbucks merchandise, baseball gloves, chewing gum paper, monster drink cans, and viewing stones. In the eyes of the average person unfamiliar with this trend, the wide variety of collections can be quite surprising. Collectibles are growing to become wildly popular topics for streaming videos and clips on Twitch and YouTube, and "bragging contests" are popping up. Live streamers are gaining popularity by showing off their collections. For example, "Room Show Off Contest방자랑대회" by YouTuber Hye-an, who has 1.52 million subscribers, drew attention for showing off a collection of frog dolls, ornaments, socks, and furniture that she collected with her mother over the span of 30 years.

Collecting is not just about the items, but also about the experiences they embody. A familiar term among people who like musicals, "the revolving door fan," is representative of those who like expanding their collection of experiences. Even during the pandemic, musical theaters were crowded thanks to these revolving door fans, who get their name from not leaving the building through the revolving door after watching a performance and instead walking back inside to rewatch the same show.

In March 2022, Interpark announced the results of the "repeat audience survey" among musical show audiences. In 2021, the highest repeat viewing of the same show by a single person was 86 times, followed by 77 and 72. The "escape room방탈출" game, which has emerged as a new playground for the younger crowd, is also among the widely collected experiences. A search for "escape room reviews" on the internet will display a long list of blog posts of professional room escapists who have completed room escapes on average more than 300 times. Escape room games are sophisticated psychological games with a wide range of levels of difficulty, genres, and durations. When someone completes the mission of escaping a room they record details of the experience, including the difficulty level, types of hints, story summary, types of activities, fear level, interior design, and outfits.

Socio-cultural Factors Behind Digging Momentum

Taking interest in other people's tastes and hobbies is not something new. But what is the socio-cultural backdrop behind this recent growth of the digging trend? The results of a survey conducted by Konan Technology which classified the frequency of the appearance of keywords such as "digging," "over-immersion과몰입," and "fandom" among 20-50-year-olds reveal two trends. First, the interest in digging is higher among the young generation in their 20s and 30s, and the interest among 40-50-year-olds is also increasing steadily over time.

First, consider the characteristics of the younger generation referred to as Generation Z. This generation sees virtual worlds as not just a form of virtual reality but a form of actual reality because games have been part of their daily routine since childhood, and they have grown up closely with digital devices. Therefore, immersing oneself in something unrealistic is much easier, and they actually enjoy the experience. They are more passionate about sci-fi and fantasy films such as *The Avengers, Harry Potter,* and *The Lord of the Rings* than any other generation. This fantasy does not stop with just reading the series of books or watching the movies but expands into a universe. It is through this lens that people can understand the phenomenon in which the Star Wars series, which has long been familiar to the older generations, has only recently grown into a wider universe of content rather than just another series. For Generation MZ, digging and over-immersion is a normal part of life, and a very important aspect of their culture.

Digging among the forty- and fifty-somethings is also increasing. Some believe it is not easy to have a new passion for something as you get older, but it would be wrong to think that digging is a culture limited to the younger generations. Since digging is simply an extension of people's open-ended search to find what they really enjoy, there is no age limit for people looking for a subject to be captivated by. As examples in the introduction show, the number of people in their 30s and 40s who enjoy Legos, which some think of as a children's game, is increasing. In other words, digging is a trend that spans generations.

The reason why the Digging Momentum trend is getting stronger and more visible is due to the power of immersion. According to psychologist and originator of the concept of "flow," Mihaly Csikszentmihalyi, the belief that a person's topic of interest has value is enough to make something meaningful. In other words, only people who have this belief are able to fully enjoy and appreciate life. People who are able to immerse themselves in their favorite topics, even for a short time during the day, will have the mental strength to overcome stress the next day.

The pandemic, escalating social conflict, and the economic crisis are among the factors behind the digging trend's spread. Anxiety is not something people can choose or control but a reality that just has to be faced and endured. Martin Seligman, the founder of positive psychology, said that there is a formula for happiness, and that it is possible to create a happy state of mind. According to Seligman's "Happiness Equation," the degree of happiness we feel is determined by the sum of our genetic predispositions and the autonomy we can control combined with external conditions. That means blaming genetics or external factors alone that one cannot control is not the right way to relieve anxiety. In unavoidable circumstances such as the pandemic, political and social unrest, and a recession, it is perhaps natural for people to find solace in the things that they have complete control over.

How does one achieve happiness? Professor Choi Incheol of the Department of Psychology at Seoul National University, who conducts research on happiness, said, "human happiness is being in a state in which there is an object of interest in a person's mind" and "a state of happiness comes when the person is ready to actively reach toward that object." Even in everyday life, during moments of extreme stress and anxiety, if there is a special interest in people's hearts that can help change their mood to happiness instantly – like a flick of a switch – then they can effectively overcome such stress in their present day lives, even if it's just for a moment. Perhaps a digger is someone who holds the key to happiness, by living with an easily accessible favorite topic inside their heart.

Outlook and Implications

As more people get serious about their own niche subject, related industries such as entertainment, content creators, and purveyors of kidult (kid+adult) toys are also growing. Furthermore, the rising influence of these diggers means their role in marketing efforts in various industries is becoming more important. In particular, the implications of this group are significant in cultivating a media strategy that requires dexterity and the social influence to make an underground trend mainstream.

Mainstream media, which used to be TV, radio, newspapers, and magazines, has now shifted to a myriad of digital channels. This means media strategy that can effectively utilize these multiple channels is becoming increasingly important. For example, entertainment group SM Entertainment plans to create an infinite "content universe" so that K-pop fans can proactively lead trends in local pop culture. The multimedia video first shown in SM's CU (Content Universe) is called "CAWMAN," an acronym for cartoons, animations, web-toons, motion graphics, avatars, and novels. This is an example of the shift where content utilizes a wide range of technologies and crosses multiple genres. To get diggers on board, companies will need to constantly provide new sources of entertainment and enjoyment. In August 2022, Kakao announced the return of "Ra-Chun Duo라춘듀오," the group formed by Kakao's popular character Ryan and his friend Chun-sik. To get to the fans who have been waiting for them to come back with new content, news of the duo's return was released on TikTok, YouTube, Instagram, and Twitter. By marketing the content in formats specialized for each platform the company was able to maximize the reception. Events held at The Hyundai Seoul, the favorite department store of Generation MZ, and at Incheon International Airport to celebrate the duo's new content are a prime example of cross-media marketing.

One final point to note is that there are still concerns about the activities of individual diggers. Excessive digging is one of them. For Digging Momentum to remain healthy, there has to be a boundary between digging and addiction. According to psychiatrist William Glasser, addiction can be classified as positive and negative addiction. Positive addiction provides emotional fulfillment, but negative addiction only provides temporary pleasure. To take advantage of the positive effects of digging, people need to set their own standards.

Digging may not be about the subject in the end, but more about us. It is difficult to draw a clear line between whether digging is an escape from reality or an immersive practice that helps people find their interests, and their selves. Seligman notes the need to distinguish between momentary pleasures and immersion that helps people grow psychologically. The key is growth. When the activity can be harmonized with daily life under the broader direction of self-improvement, digging can become the momentum for real progress in people's lives.

Jumbly
Generation Alpha

A generation of true digital natives starts with children whose first word was "Alexa," not "Mom." This is "Generation Alpha," born after 2010, which follows Generation Z born between 1995 and 2009. Since 'Z' is the final letter of the alphabet, the letter-naming system was reset to the beginning, hence "Generation Alpha." This generation does not merely follow Generation Z, but rather symbolizes the emergence of a completely new tribe. Generation Alpha was born to millennial parents born in the 1980s, who themselves kicked off a new generation. Generation Alpha was raised in completely new times and are now growing up under the influence of the pandemic. Generation Alpha, or "Gen Alpha" for short, is characterized by the respect they hold for one another's uniqueness and the belief that each person has a very special identity amidst this jumbly generation of individuals. They tend to be egocentric and believe that the self is the most important value, so everyone considers themselves to be some sort of celebrity or architect. Thus, they believe anyone can easily become an influencer, using TikTok as their main social media platform. They are open to learning new subjects like coding. In addition, they are interested in learning about the economy and finance. After Covid 19 struck, many activities were conducted online in spaces such as Zoom, but Gen Alpha craves more offline activities. Compared to the previous generation, Gen Alpha seems to be growing up amid unprecedented convenience and a wholly digital environment. However, when asked the question "Are you happy?" the answer is not so straightforward. The group's happiness index score is the lowest in the OECD, and polarization through the digital divide is widening. Parents, schools, and society as a whole need to pay more attention to the happiness of this newest, jumbly generation. The future of Gen Alpha is the future of Korea.

Generation MZ is the most frequently cited generation as a key measure of social change. The "M" is for "millennials," the alias for Generation Y, which refers to those born between 1980 and 1994. Generation Z refers to those born between 1995 and 2009. So, what comes after MZ? There is no letter of the alphabet that follows from X-Y-Z, so we go back to the beginning, with "Generation Alpha." These are children born after 2010, under the age of 13. Generations are divided by a new name every 15 years, so until 2024, it will remain the age of Generation Alpha.

There is a reason for this generation being named "Alpha" and not simply "A." "From alpha to omega," (the first and last letters of the Greek alphabet) is another way of saying "from beginning to end," so it can be seen as a metaphor for the birth of a completely new tribe, not merely the generation that follows Generation Z. As in the expression "alpha girl," the word suggests excellence, which applies to the characteristics of the whole generation. Generation Alpha's parents are millennials born in the 1980s, who kicked off their respective generation. Generation Alpha, or "Gen Alpha" for short, was raised in completely different times and are now growing up under the influence of the pandemic. It was reported in the UK that the first words of an 18-month-old child were not "Mom" or "Dad," but "Alexa" – the activation word for Amazon's smart speaker. They are true digital natives who have lived with digital devices from birth.

There may be one or two Gen Alpha members in our lives, but how well do we understand them? Let's solve the following problem. Here are two true or false statements.

Statement 1. Gen Alpha makes more purchases online and in the metaverse than at offline stores.

Statement 2. Gen Alpha will use KakaoTalk more often than text messaging.

Both statements are false.

Explanation 1. When we think of Gen Alpha, we imagine them playing with Robux on gaming platform Roblox and using virtual currencies, but in reality, they make up a higher proportion of offline purchases than any other generation. Why? When purchases are made online, it's usually the parents who collect them from the front door first. Gen Alphas don't want their parents to see what they've bought, so they prefer to just go to the store to make a purchase.

Explanation 2. Parents often block KakaoTalk from being installed on their children's phones to keep them from excessively chatting with friends, and to protect them from bullying and cybercrime. So, Gen Alphas keep in touch with their friends through text messages or Facebook DMs.

Gen Alpha has not received much attention compared to other generations because they are still minors and their numbers are smaller compared to that of previous generations. However, they have deep pockets. Their parents, grandparents on both sides, aunts and uncles give them generous allowances. In particular, millennial parents are a key driver of their children's purchasing power because they are lavish with their kids. By 2023, the "oldest" Gen Alphas will have graduated from elementary school. Middle school students will then hit puberty and start being rebellious. We have reached a point where some serious investigation into Gen Alpha is called for – to clarify our jumbly conceptions of who they really are. Gen Alpha, the true beginning of the digital and mobile generation, is here, living in a world that is completely different from the childhoods of older generations.

The Dreams and Identities of Gen Alpha

"My dream is to become a YouTuber with millions of followers. I need to learn how to run a channel and increase my subscribers to become more popular with my friends."

- interview with a 12-year-old elementary school student

The most common aspiration of Gen Alpha is to become a YouTuber with millions of followers, not a doctor, lawyer, actor, or athlete. As far as they are concerned, YouTubers are the perfect mentors. If you offer to teach them anything, they will say, "I'll just watch YouTube and figure it out." Video editing cram schools are crowded with elementary school students. This is because unlike in the past, when other children with good grades or athletes were popular role models, influencers with masses of followers are much more popular today. There are even YouTube academy lectures which cater specifically to elementary school students.

The etymology of the English word "generation" is the Latin *generatus*, "to beget, produce," which itself comes from *genus*, "race, or kind." Elementary school students these days are not an extension of the older generations but are a newly begotten and completely different tribe: Generation Alpha.

Everyone is a celebrity

He's a good dancer, at the level of a master. Some kids aren't good at Roblox, but they can speak English well. Not just "well" but at the level of a native speaker. I think the level of expertise by kids in each field has improved significantly. Also, the fields of specialization are diverse; no child is good at everything, and it feels like everyone has their own specific strengths.

- Kim XX, who is raising a second grader,
during a focus group discussion among parents of Gen Alpha students
at Seoul National University's Consumer Trend Analysis Center

Having the highest grades in school had once been a common goal for people over 40. In middle and high schools in the 1980s and 1990s, students were ranked from 1st to 100th based on their grades, and the lists were posted on the walls of classrooms. During those times, studying hard and getting good grades was of the utmost importance. Regardless of the student being talented at dancing or singing, low grades meant the student was a problem child. That was when the word *"umchina*엄친아*"* – an abbreviation of 엄마 친구 아들 (son of Mom's friend) – was coined. There always seemed to be a child at every school who was described as, "that picture perfect son of Mom's friend who not only gets top grades, but also has a good personality and is a great athlete." An object of envy and jealousy of average students, there was always that one child who had the upper hand among peers.

Now, for Gen Alpha, the concept of having the highest grades in the whole school or being that one stellar *umchina*, doesn't work like it used to. Rather, those high achievers tend to be less popular. Instead, being good in just one field, be it running or badminton or something of the like, is enough to gain recognition. Gen Alpha accepts that everyone has a different personality and abilities. Rather than giving up hope because of poor grades, the new generation just acknowledges their differences and does the best they can in their own areas. However, due to increased self-centeredness, they are also a generation that believes they are each the most important person in the world. That underlies Gen Alpha's belief that "each and every one of us is a celebrity." And because many are an only child due to the low birth rate and don't experience competition from siblings, Gen Alphas develop a "main character fantasy."

From a psychological standpoint, the development of egocentrism during infancy and early childhood, in which children believe that the world revolves around them, is naturally quite strong. They have a strong tendency to believe that they are very special and that their feelings and thoughts are fundamentally different from other people's – what child psychologist David Elkind coined the "personal fable." "Mom, how would you know how I feel? No one knows how I feel!" is a common expression of this personal fable. Furthermore, many fall into the illusion that they are the main characters on a theatrical stage and that others are spectators watching them. A girl fixing her hair in front of the mirror for over an hour, or a boy dressed in flashy clothes, is a manifestation of being conscious of an imaginary audience which, along with personal fables, is rooted in self-centeredness. Believing one is the center of the world is perhaps a natural developmental step in growing up.

TikTok, the social network service frequently used by Gen Alpha, has achieved great success by perfectly catering to this generational trait. Among Korean teenagers, TikTok usage surpasses that of KakaoTalk and Naver, with total usage time of TikTok hitting 1.94 billion hours per month, exceeding that of KakaoTalk (1.86 billion hours) and Naver (1.14 billion hours) according to a sample survey of Korean teenagers. Experts see the main reason behind TikTok's explosive growth among teenagers as being due to TikTok's algorithm, which accurately caters to the desires of teenagers who seek to be celebrities or influencers. YouTube, Facebook, and Instagram are platforms which are driven by the number of subscribers each person has, making it difficult for teenagers to compete with powerful influencers that already have millions of followers. With TikTok, however, there are more opportunities. On the "For You" page, which is the home screen for all users, random videos based on number of likes are displayed. This gives virtually anyone the chance to get exposure through this page, and once featured on this page, people who are not influencers can easily get a visibility boost in a very short period of time. TikTok's recommendation of hundreds and even thousands of videos greatly increases the probability that an unknown TikTokker can become a star one day, which is significantly attractive for teenagers who dream of becoming celebrities.

This algorithm allows TikTokkers to captivate users while being true to their own selves. In other words, if a video gives the impression of being too well put together – looking too perfect or made up at a professional level – it can have a negative effect. It is the natural charm of a person that attracts the most attention on this platform. In contrast, other social platforms require a certain degree of professional-grade production skills for users to differentiate themselves from the rest. Gen Alphas' unique way of expressing themselves with the aid of TikTok's recommendation algorithm, and their culture of appreciating the individuality of other people, have come together seamlessly to establish TikTok as the dominant platform for teenagers.

We are architects! Mastering mechanisms over technique

Unlike the past, when students studied in classrooms with teachers and worksheets, Gen Alpha is more accustomed to taking virtual and online classes with AI teachers on tablet PCs. Thus, learning how to code has been a natural progression and is now increasingly becoming a necessity. In August 2022, the government announced a target of cultivating a million digital experts. While there are relevant subjects taught at middle and high school levels, having digital-centric education available for younger children is just as important. The goal is to increase the number of hours of IT classes by including them in elementary school elective courses, expanding middle and high school course offerings, and moving towards required coding courses for elementary and middle schools. Coding education can also be accessed through AI home-study materials. One prime example is "Reading How to Code독서코딩" for young children. It is a curriculum that helps develop coding literacy, computational thinking, and creative problem-solving skills through stories that include a range of coding material.

Coding itself is not the main focus. Coding techniques and technology are constantly changing. Simply learning how to use a specific coding language or software cannot be the end goal to cultivate digital experts. The vital competency taught is the ability to understand the underlying operating principles. Understanding the foundational knowledge is essential to building and designing programs. Professor Art Markman, a cognitive psychologist and author of *Smart Thinking: How to Think Big, Innovate and Outperform Your Rivals*, has said that "understanding the principles of work" is the key to smart thinking. A toilet handle, for example, is connected to a cable that pulls up the flapper at the bottom of the water tank. The flapper takes the pressure off the valve, then the water in the tank begins to drain out. Knowing the basic operation mechanism of the toilet is an example of operational thinking. This is the basis for smarter thinking: widening the scope of making better judgments based on broader knowledge. The best way to understand these types of principles is to design and build something oneself.

Parents of Gen Alpha know better than anyone that understanding the underlying principle is more important than memorizing methodology. The key is to be an architect who can see the bigger picture and build anything, rather than to be just a programmer. Thus, it is crucial to provide more diverse learning opportunities in the real world to build experiences as opposed to unfettered and unfocused time spent online. The act of making and building something can serve as both play and an educational method in the development of students' minds.

Finance, a Compulsory Subject for Gen Alpha

As mentioned in *Consumer Trend Insights 2021 and 2022,* the "Money-friendly Generation" and "Money Rush" trends have now become mainstream. Millennial parents who are familiar with financial topics do not just focus on classroom education and coding. Perhaps the most important ability in life is having an interest in economics and investment.

Level 1. Learning how to spend – going Dutch when eating out with family

La El Kim: *"I have to pay for all the food I eat."*
Hong Jin-kyung: *"When I used to pay for everything, including when we eat out, the kids didn't need pocket money, so I would find pocket money lying about on the floor in their rooms. Now I just increase their allowances and make them pay for everything separately. We also go Dutch when eating out."*
-Part of an interview with TV personality Hong Jin-kyung and her daughter

This is part of an interview between TV personality Hong Jin-kyung and her daughter La El Kim (born in 2010 and who was 12 years old at the time of the interview). Hong's unique financial teaching method for her daughter, who has yet to appreciate the value of her allowance, is notable. Financial education is based on the concept that wants are infinite and resources are limited. A key challenge for Gen Alpha is that they must be selective about what they buy. The older generations, who always lacked pocket money, had no choice but to be good at controlling their spending; but the affluent allowance-rich Gen Alphas must learn to control their spending on their own initiative.

The value of money perceived by children is different from that of adults. For adults, 30,000 won is money that can only be earned by working, but for many children the same 30,000 won is just money received when allowance day comes around, or money that they get from relatives during family gatherings. Easy money is spent easily. In order for children to understand the value of money, it's best to have them experience earning money. For example, children are given pocket money in return for chores done at home. More families are offering their children unique jobs at home, such as a barista who makes coffee for the family every morning, or a DJ who plays the music in the house, naturally providing financial training at home.

After understanding the value of money, it's time to learn how to spend it. Training is needed to make the most rational choice among many options, and to then let the rest go. Gen Alphas, who grew up amid an abundance of resources, need specific training to ask themselves, "What choice would give me the greatest satisfaction?" or "What choice would make me happier?" and to learn how to allocate resources efficiently. Such measures are necessary because Gen Alphas have grown accustomed to online purchases where there is no physical person that stands between them and free consumption.

As the methods of consumption have diversified, the age

at which spending starts has become younger. Gen Alphas, who are still young and prone to impulsive spending, are newly minted consumers who need to actively learn how to spend in moderation. Children who make significant purchases in the metaverse are not uncommon. Among Gen Alphas in the US, YouTubers that upload "shopping spree" videos of stationery and toys have drawn considerable attention.

Level 2. Teaching students how to invest and manage – "Kidpreneurs"

Once spending in moderation is mastered, the next level is learning how to invest. In recent years, interest in investing has grown. As the keyword "Money Rush" in *Consumer Trend Insights 2022* illustrates, investments which were once limited to stocks and real estate have broadened to cryptocurrencies, NFTs, art, and foreign currencies.

This in turn has led to children's interest in learning financial subjects. Now, it is not uncommon to see parents and grandparents buying stocks for children instead of giving them pocket money. 91,000 new stock accounts for minors were opened in 2021 and 17,000 in the first quarter of 2022 alone, according to Korea Investment & Securities. Also notable is that the sales of financial education books targeting the younger age group have also increased. About 50 children's economic study books have been published in

2022, more than double that of last year, with sales increasing by 89%. Another impressive feat is that *Children Paying Taxes*세금 내는 아이들 ranked 58th on the bestseller list among children's books.

The most effective way to experience market dynamics firsthand is to "become the boss." In recent years, an increasing number of teenagers are starting their own businesses online. Setting up a shopping mall to sell items they made, operating a YouTube and other social media channels, and marketing their products are all part of the process. Items range from stationery to clothing and accessories.

Searching for keywords such as "teenage boss" or "student boss" on YouTube brings up many clips detailing the startup process. The topics are diverse, including: how to obtain a business registration certificate; how to operate a shopping mall and make products; and even where to purchase raw materials.

Clips that answer viewers' questions related to startups are also popular. These cover how to open an online store, difficulties in day-to-day operation, and challenges of working as a minor. Another reason for the increase in these teenage bosses is that virtual classes have increased after the pandemic, giving students flexibility in using their spare time for other activities. Some examples of what they originally made as a hobby and then go on to sell are accessories, manicure materials, and stickers. The expansion of services and tools that make it easy to open online shopping malls, as well as the many small- and medium-sized shopping platforms that have appeared on the scene, have all helped to lower any entry barriers.

What Does Gen Alpha Do for Fun?

Although Gen Alpha is known as the representative digital native, they do not necessarily hang out in the digital world. They prefer a well-balanced combination of the physical and digital worlds. Zenly, a popular app among teenagers, is a prime example. Zenly is a location-based social media platform where users can share their current location with friends in real time and exchange messages. Through Zenly, users share data such as where they currently are and where they are headed. The two main hangouts for Gen Alpha are Zoom and Daiso.

Study and hang out with friends
while screen sharing on Zoom

"A friend I used to go to kindergarten with has moved away, but I still study English with this friend three times a week on Zoom. I read and study for 30-40 minutes. After we finish reading, we watch slime videos on a shared YouTube screen

together. That's how I study and play with my friends."

- Third grader during an interview

with Seoul National University Trend Analysis Center

This is an example of an elementary school student who still hangs out with a friend who moved away by sharing a screen on Zoom. For Gen Alphas who are accustomed to video calls, physical distance is no obstacle. Most Gen Alphas are comfortable in the virtual world, with the most representative place being the metaverse.

Roblox is a leading gaming platform in the shift to the metaverse. Roblox is not a single game, but a virtual world in which several games are played. When a user uploads a game, other users can play for free. Users choose an avatar for all the games on the platform. In other words, the user can go back and forth between games with one avatar. Because of these characteristics, Roblox has become a game where the relationship between users is crucial. A friend in one game transfers over to another game as a friend as well. Users can see what games Roblox friends are playing now and can join in. Just as children play with their friends in real life, they play with their friends online in the virtual game world.

The games on Roblox are not sophisticated enough for adults. The structure and settings are simple because anyone, including young children, can make and upload a game.

Thus, 25% of Roblox users are under the age of 9, and 29% say they are between 9 and 12 years old. For this age group, making new friends and hanging out together is much more important than flashy game stories and graphics. Roblox is becoming more than just a virtual space for children to play simple games for hours.

After school, a popular routine

Children playing on the playground of apartment complexes have become a rare sight in recent years. True, many play-grounds were closed due to the pandemic, but they did not fit the lifestyle of Gen Alpha to begin with. The playground, which was a common gathering place for youngsters of the older generations, is no longer important for Gen Alpha. There is little time to go out and play, and the pollution and extreme weather has become a deterrent to playing outdoors. However, for Gen Alpha today, there are various offline activities that replace the playground. After school, looking at things at Daiso다이소 store, taking pictures with friends at the self-portrait studio Life4Cuts인생네컷, eating mala hot pot마라탕, and chatting over bubble tea is their idea of a perfect day.

In childhood, kids cafés were a place to meet other chil-dren, but when they became elementary school students, the neighborhood stationery store took over as a meeting hub. It is not a stretch to say that the local stationery stores, with their wide array of products from toys to video games, is a cultural space for elementary school students. These shops have long been a favorite, but one thing that has changed is that many of today's stationery shops are unmanned. From the children's point of view, this automated shop is a welcome change because they can come and go freely and take their time looking at products and playing games without having to mind an adult onlooker. For example, automated stationery store Let's Play Stationery문구야 놀자, which opened in November 2020, started recruiting franchisees in March 2021 and expanded their stores nationwide to 120 locations within a year. Sales grew 200-300% compared to 2020.

There is another favorite shopping center for elementary school students: popular household goods chain Daiso. Now considered a department store for elementary school students, Daiso allows students with a few thousand won of spare pocket money to shop while exploring the massive array of products without employees pressuring them or watching over them. This has become the place students stop by whenever they have some time before or after school. From stationery to daily necessities and basic cosmetics, shopping at Daiso has become something of a ritual. Elementary school students spend so much here that if you analyze Daiso's top selling items by age group, the trends of elementary school students become clearly visible. In the first half of 2021, the top consumed items by Gen Alpha were hobby items, including decorative stickers and sorting baskets. Daiso recently opened an official TikTok account and has been actively marketing to Gen Alpha, offering short-form video content that introduces their products to elementary school students in an entertaining way.

Turbulent life experiences since 2010

Society is changing rapidly. Just like Moore's Law, which states that the sophistication of semiconductor technology doubles every two years, in terms of technology, the same changes that mankind has accumulated thus far seem to be doubling every two years. In times that are not just changing fast, but also accelerating exponentially, the 14 years' worth of change experienced by Gen Alpha is equal to what older generations have experienced over several decades. The table below summarizes their experiences based on those born in 2012, who are currently 10 years old.

What is notable about the experiences of Gen Alphas is that they were born and grew up amidst a number of big changes: the low birth rate becoming evident; video platforms like YouTube becoming mainstream; work-life balance becoming a debated issue; the growing influence of Korea's cultural sector on the global scene; and the continuous breakthroughs in cutting-edge technologies such as arti-

〈 Life experiences of those born in 2012 〉

Year	Age	Event
2012	0	Psy's 'Gangnam Style' craze ranks No. 1 on YouTube
2014	2	Multiple progressive education superintendents are elected Sewol ferry disaster occurs
2016	4	The artificial intelligence age begins (AlphaGo vs. Lee Sedol)
2018	6	Korea's working-age population shrinks for the first time The 52-hour work week begins
2020	8	Remote classes start due to the pandemic BTS ranks No. 1 on the Billboard charts; *Parasite* wins 4 Academy awards
2022	10	Students return to the classroom

ficial intelligence. And the biggest change was undoubtedly when they entered school during a global pandemic, being required to wear masks and experiencing limited face-to-face contact.

In order to understand the characteristics of a certain generation, it is necessary to look at the life experiences shared by that age group. The period from birth to age 14 is a period of very rapid change, growth, and development.

Since Gen Alphas are still minors, the context in which they have grown up, their parents, family, and school environment should all provide the best understanding of the group. Let's take a look at the influencing context that gives Gen Alpha its unique characteristics.

Precious children amid a low birth rate

Gen Alphas are known to be egocentric and to have a strong tendency to come up with their own answers rather than looking to others as a guide. These characteristics are heavily influenced by a low birth rate. As the school-age population shrinks, the number of elementary school students have declined dramatically. Even in some of the most populated areas, there are less than 30 children per classroom. For the older generations who grew up taking classes in packed classrooms filled with 60 or more students, this is a dramatic change. As in the past, when growing up in an extended family of four to six members or more, as well as attending large classes, conformity and valuing the group over the individual is given higher importance. But now, smaller households have become the norm and the birth rate is in decline with the number of deaths now outpacing births. Despite the declining number of school-age children, the market targeting children is growing. As the birth rate declines, the trend to give children more pocket money is growing stronger. It is only natural for Gen Alphas to be highly self-centered when they grow up with all adult attention focused on them.

Characteristics of millennial parents

Parents have a dominant influence on the development of a child. Thus, it is important to look deeper into some of the characteristics of the millennial generation, the parents of Gen Alpha. Their view of childcare differs from past generations. Millennials have received a form of intensive parenting during childhood. With just one or two children in the household, they received ample education and grew into a generation that has a higher level of education than any other generation. Due to this background, a common characteristic of millennials is narcissism. Millennials prefer not to follow the path pursued by the older generations, but rather a life of self-satisfaction.

Due to the effects of self-centeredness, many millennial parents have grown to have an aversion to education based on just memorization, and their perception of success is different from that of older generations. When asked the question "What does it mean to have succeeded in raising children well in our society?" the answer "Growing up doing what they want to do" was selected as number one (25.1%). "Growing up as a person with good character" was second (22.4%), and "Finding a good job" came in third (21.3%), according to a 2021 survey of 4,000 adult men and women by the Korea Educational Development Institute. The answer "Finding a good job" had been the number-one answer for four straight years from 2015 to 2018. This was the first year the rankings had changed suggesting that parents' attitudes about the measure of success are changing.

Another important characteristic of millennial parents is that women do not automatically choose the path of full-time housewives as was common with the older generations. Of all newlyweds, 52% are working as dual-income earners, which is a 2.9% increase from a year ago. In 2020, for the first time since records were compiled, the proportion of dual-income earners was higher than single-income households for all years of marriage from the first year to the fifth. Meanwhile, millennial dads are more active in sharing household chores and teaching their children than the fathers of the previous generation, who were largely unconcerned about their children's education. As such, it is inevitable that Gen Alphas born from parents who have built a strong identity and career under their own name embody a high level of self-centeredness.

The dark side of the pandemic

The impact of the pandemic is significant. When working from home and virtual learning were concurrently in session, the home resembled a warzone. Many parents complained about the lack of playtime options their children had –

and the lack of breaks parents had from their children. But it was an especially difficult time for the children. One in three elementary school students experienced depression or anxiety, according to a survey on the effects of the prolonged pandemic on student mental health. Among the lower grades of elementary school, 25.4% of respondents said that they became more depressed than before the pandemic and 23.8% reported suffering from anxiety. Academic habits have been adversely affected as students were not able to go to school for most of the past three years. In particular, the proportion of students who answered that they spend more time using the internet and smartphones was very large.

The most serious fallout from the pandemic for Gen Alpha is not the virus itself but the negative effects of wearing facial masks for prolonged periods. As the use of masks has become a daily requirement, the emotional and social development of infants and young children has been hindered. A survey of directors, teachers, and parents of public daycare centers in Seoul and Gyeonggi Province in April 2022 showed that three quarters of the respondents were concerned that masks had decreased children's exposure to language learning and developmental opportunities. A growing number of children are yet to say simple phrases even when they are over the age of two while some others still cannot pronounce certain letters even though they are already six or seven years old. Some middle and high school students skip lunch because they don't want to take off their masks. More children are having trouble reading other people's emotions because they are out less and do not have experience reading the expressions of their friends and teachers. Exactly how long these aftereffects will last is of great concern.

Outlook and Implications

It is said that there was a time when the phrase "poor kid with perfect attendance" was widely used among elementary school students. Once a symbol of integrity and hard work, having a perfect attendance rate has now become a sign of poverty, essentially signaling that the student had not had the chance to travel abroad. As mentioned in the "Disappearing Average" trend, polarization is emerging as a big problem even among Gen Alpha.

In particular, the rising digital divide is the most troubling development. The digital divide refers to the disparity between individuals, families, and regions at different socio-economic levels in relation to access to communication and internet use. A survey conducted by the Korea Youth Policy Institute on fourh to sixth graders and their parents in 2020 showed a striking difference in the level of available infrastructure for remote learning based on the parents' financial and educational background. Children's access to digital devices and their ability to use software are also significantly affected by their parents' socioeconomic status. Qualitatively speaking, the lower the socioeconomic status of the parents and the lower the adequacy of home guidance for their children's media use, the higher the rate of overall media misuse among children.

But those on the privileged side of the digital divide, the digital natives who have been exposed to the digital world from birth, are at high risk of addiction without knowing it. When eating out with their families, these digital natives are so used to watching YouTube and cartoons on mobile phones, believing from a young age that they will eventually become YouTubers, and then TikTok influencers. But even for adults, finding the appropriate balance between reality and the digital world can be difficult. There is a high risk that the Gen Alpha will spend hours and hours shopping online or glued to social media without even realizing it. It is even difficult for adults to withstand the lure of big tech companies that reel in users with the aid of big data and algorithms. But it is Gen Alphas who are at a vulnerable age where both avoiding and managing addiction becomes particularly challenging, so adult guidance is crucial.

Societal problems related to raising Gen Alpha in a highly digital environment are growing too. The issue of personal data and privacy is especially serious. The sheer amount of personal information floating around on the internet that has amassed since Gen Alpha's birth poses an increasing risk. Parents upload pictures of their children's life on social media to such an extent that it's warranted a new term: "sharenting" (share + parenting). There is also the ongoing risk of misuse of this personal information. Celebrities that are caught in scandals due to inappropriate posts they wrote during their school days is a commonly reported issue — a side effect of troves of information being permanently displayed on the internet. The fact that these issues should be addressed by the Personal Information Protection Act is even more problematic due to the fact that laws lack consideration for younger age groups who are yet to actively exercise their privacy rights.

Gen Alphas may want to hide their past immature behaviors once they become adults. The "right to be forgotten" is crucial. Even in the United States, which emphasizes freedom of expression, some state laws guarantee the right of minors to "be forgotten" through the provision of "disclosure of information on children." In Korea, the right to request corrections and deletions of inaccurate personal information are clearly stipulated. Yet when it comes to external links to posts by unspecified authors, there are times when the right to be forgotten is not fully guaranteed. As the digital generation becomes mainstream, coming up with a system that can solve related problems is an increasingly pressing task.

Compared to previous generations, Gen Alpha is growing up amid a digital environment that offers unprecedented convenience, but when it comes to the question, "Are you happy?" the answer is not so straightforward. The happiness index for children and adolescents in Korea ranked last among OECD countries at 22nd, according to the results of a recent study: "Korean Children and Youth Happiness Index." As the saying goes, "Children are the mirror image of adults." The survey results may be reflecting the reality of Korea, which ranks at the bottom of the world's happiness index. The happiness of this newest, jumbly generation should be a bigger priority for parents, schools, and society in general. After all, the future of Gen Alpha will soon be the future of Korea.

선제적 대응기술

Unveiling Proactive Technology

06 : 30
THU 08 JUN

32° 34°
25°

Good morning

Technology makes life easier. Yet until now, for technology to get to the stage of making life more convenient, users have had to bear with the inconvenience of properly utilizing it and setting it up based on their own requirements. But we are now at a stage in which technology is able to identify necessary functions on its own and provide the services proactively, in advance. In other words, technology analyzes user patterns to suggest ways for us to make better use of it, as well as going a step further by executing a function before the user expresses the need. The final step is creating a solution before the user even realizes a solution was needed. *Consumer Trend Insights 2023* would like to call this technology that relieves users of the inconvenience of having to tell it what to do "Proactive Technology."

Proactive Technology is already a part of daily life for many users and the scope of its application is expanding rapidly. The level of how proactive a technology is can be largely classified in the following stages: providing information preemptively so that the user can choose among the choices; automatically customizing functions according to past user data; and predicting user needs in advance and performing the functions even before the user acts. Proactive Technology is expected to catch on rapidly in the public sector as well. For Proactive Technology to be widely used, it must be able to analyze user behavior and accumulate significant amounts of data sets. Moreover, it must extract insights and respond in a timely manner. A deep understanding of consumer behavior linked with products that provide proactive assistance to consumers is equally important for further uptake of the technology. The competitive edge of Proactive Technology will be determined by the first movers who provide more suitable solutions to problems that have not yet occurred by figuring out the needs of consumers that they themselves have not yet even realized.

*W*hen a user is on the phone while standing in front of and operating an ATM, a warning message appears on the screen saying, "Please stop talking on your mobile phone before making a transaction in order to prevent financial accidents." A little bit later, when a user whose face is covered with sunglasses and a hat stands in front of the ATM, the machine displays the message: "Please take off your hat and sunglasses."

This ATM is equipped with abnormal behavior detection AI installed by Shinhan Bank in branches which have a high proportion of elderly customers so as to prevent crimes such as voice phishing. Internal data experts and companies specializing in AI analyzed the behavior types of normal and abnormal banking transactions at the ATM and used machine learning to come up with the system. This is a representative example of the direction recent technological developments are headed. ATMs are no longer just machines that people use to withdraw cash – they can also understand the intention, situation, and context of the user and provide relevant functions.

Technology is everywhere. As Homo sapiens evolved, technological advances have been the reason behind humans' ability to enjoy a safe and convenient lifestyle. Technology exists to make people's lives more convenient. Yet until now, for technology to make life convenient, users have had to undergo the inconvenience of properly utilizing it and setting it up based on their own needs. This was necessary as the technology available for commercial use was designed as a "general purpose product" with the average consumer in mind. Indeed, there are some products that are highly customized and tailored to individual needs. However, each of these customized products requires a separate manufacturing process, making these options relatively expensive, as well as inconvenient given the user must adjust each specific setting to their tastes.

Recently, technology that understands user context and intention and that provides timely solutions are becoming increasingly common. The evolution of this technology is apparent in many fields, particularly the construction industry where "smart living" technologies are driving change. For example, the "Welcome to Raemian" system, which is used in Samsung C&T's apartment brand Raemian래미안, turns on the lights and displays updates when a person enters the living room. The software even determines what is appropriate for the same user for that time of day; for example, when it is time to wake up, the living room lights turn on and the home display system shows information needed to start the day, such as the day's weather. If the software determines that the user is returning home, the screen displays a list of visitors who rang the bell in the user's absence, or the latest public notices for the apartment complex.

As such, technology that analyzes customers' usage patterns is able to provide better solutions, and furthermore, performs a function for users even before they express what they need, ultimately creating a solution before users even realize a solution was needed. *Consumer Trend Insights 2023* would like to call this technology that relieves users of the inconvenience of having to express their needs "Proactive Technology." This technology, when applied to products, analyzes the user's situation and context to make life easier.

Proactive Technology differs from existing technology that simply focuses on customization. Personalization focused on seeing each customer as a unique user, whereas Proactive Technology further breaks down that one user's profile along the multiple contexts that the user may experience over the years. One person's preferred music playlists can vary on weekdays and holidays. And even on the same day, that person's mood on the way to and from work can vary and trigger different playlists. The target is not just one customer with one user profile. The era of hyper-personalized services means a user's profile can be expanded tenfold, or even a hundredfold, to accommodate the multiple contexts they find themselves in.

Proactive Technology is an extension of the sequence of technological trends described in the *Consumer Trend Insights* series. Consumers respond well to how much a particular technology actually enriches their lives. This concept, which spawned the keyword "Calm Tech" in the 2017 edition describes the rise of invisible and quiet technology and how such low-profile technology can be successfully adopted. The adoption of data-driven decision-making processes was the driving factor behind the keyword "Data Intelligence" in the 2019 edition, which refers to intelligence derived from using a combination of data processing and decision-making technology to provide consumer-tailored responses. And "Hyper-personalization Technology," which was a keyword of 2020, converts all the situations and possible outcomes at customer contact points into datasets that can be analyzed using machine learning algorithms, which is then used to communicate with consumers through various mediums. What we call "Proactive Technology" is the culmination of a long-term evolution of technology in a consumer-oriented direction that has now reached maturity.

The act of purchasing a product is a fleeting moment, but the time it is used is much longer. The purpose of consumers buying things and using technology is largely to improve their quality of life. Therefore, the evolution of technology in a direction that maximizes the utilization of products without the user specifically having to ask for those changes is perhaps a natural progression. It is no longer enough to try to get buyers to purchase a product on the grounds that it is tailored to the consumer or even to make a product after the consumer's needs are recognized. Just as important is analyzing consumer behavior to offer a proactive and suitable response at the exact time the user needs arise.

Proactive Technology leaves no gap when it comes to catering to consumer needs. As a result, the user may not even be immediately aware that the feature or function they just used was good or useful. This is because the ultimate goal of technology is to be so natural to the point the user is not aware of its existence. This allows users the ability to focus on more important things without having to sweat the small stuff. Let's take a look at the various aspects of Proactive Technology that will quietly yet dramatically change consumers' lives.

Classification According to Application Level

#1 An alarm flashes suddenly displaying an alert that "the twelfth grader has arrived" to a family member enjoying a theater-like experience of a movie on a large-screen TV. When the family member yells "twelfth grade mode" to the AI speaker,

the TV turns off, the study room lights turn on automatically, and the air purifier switches to stealth mode, creating a quiet home atmosphere perfect for studying. Only after the high school daughter enters the house and her room, which is illuminated by a LED stand, does the rest of the family put on wireless earphones and continue watching the movie.

- From <Samsung Electronics SmartThings Daily Series>

#2 *A passerby comes upon a road under construction, takes a picture with his smartphone, and uploads it to the K-Guard app. Shortly after a notification appears on the phones of other passersby in the vicinity and informs them of the dangerous situation in real time. The K-Guard app warns people to be careful that the area is under construction before anyone reaches the dangerous spots.*

The first example is part of a marketing video showcasing Samsung Electronics' device connection experience as if it were a real-life scenario. It shows the company's goals to expand the utility of its existing technology to create an immersive, seamless overall customer experience so that users can create the daily lifestyle they want, which goes far beyond simply connecting products. The second example is the K-Guard app developed by the Electronics and Telecommunications Research Institute. This app was developed to warn people in real time of 11 types of dangers in daily life, including floods, fires, and missing persons. It works by no-tifying users of the dangers that other users have submitted in the vicinity. It is expected to contribute to the safety of the community by notifying people of dangers in real time and, in most cases, well in advance to keep them safe.

Proactive Technology is already a part of people's daily lives, and the scope of its application is widening. The level of how proactive a technology is can be largely classified in the following stages: providing information preemptively so that the user can choose among the choices; automatically customizing functions according to past user data; and pre-dicting user needs in advance and performing the functions even before the user makes a request. Each of these stages is inextricably linked rather than being three distinct stages, and they are classified according to which of the three stages was most used to get results closest to users' preferences.

Stage 1. Supply information

LG Electronics introduced "Proactive Service," a proactive function to keep home appliances maintained in their op-timal state. The PCC (Proactive Customer Care) service, which was first launched in the US market, monitors the state of the product in real time with a sensor installed inside the home appliance and sends the data it has gathered to a cloud server for analysis using AI technology. If a problem with the product is detected, such as whether the washing machine is set up on a level ground, the hot water hose is properly connected, the temperature inside the refrigerator is abnormally high, or the outdoor unit of the air conditioner is overheating, it notifies users through an app, e-mail, or text message. It also provides information such as when a washing machine needs internal cleaning, when a water purifier installed within a refrigerator needs a filter change, and how to solve temperature issues by identifying customer usage patterns. The technology improves user experience by providing contextual information and suggestions after identifying the current status, issues, and severity of problems of home appliances.

The most fundamental and practical application of Proactive Technology is to provide timely information that is customized to the situation. Technology that analyzes context is installed in the product, and the results are relayed to the user. The key is that preemptive information customized to the situation on hand is made available to the user as a proactive measure instead of just offering after care service and management after a breakdown or failure.

When ordering food through a delivery app, the most important thing consumers care about is when the food will arrive. Since users typically order while hungry, the arrival time of the meal is a sensitive issue. In response, food delivery service Baedal Minjok^{배달의민족} determines the time it takes for each step, from time of receipt of order, to cooking, to start of delivery, and to completion of delivery, providing the total estimated time of delivery and informing the waiting users of what to expect, ultimately satisfying their expected needs in advance. Once the restaurant inputs the cooking time, the estimated delivery time is calculated by taking into account past data, including driver pickup times and the distance between the home address and the restaurant. By calculating and providing the total delivery time in advance through a customized system, the once opaque waiting time has transformed into a more accurate, quantifiable time frame. Should the actual delivery time take longer than the estimated delivery time, Baedal Minjok offers a coupon. Even when deliveries take longer than the displayed estimated time, as users receive monetary compensation their satisfaction with the service remains high.

Cosmetics retailer Sephora has received attention by installing a "digital mirror" created in cooperation with interactive solution provider Wildbytes in its flagship store in Madrid. When a customer looks into the mirror, the mirror identifies the customer's gender, age group, and personal preferences. In addition, other information such as the current season, weather, and products trending in real-time in Madrid are combined in the system's software to suggest makeup, skin care, and perfume recommendations. This is the most widely available form of Proactive Technology, which recommends products by gauging the customer's current status and context in advance before the customer has time to think about which product to choose.

Technology that provides information tailored to a consumer based on their smartphone location is also widely used. US-developed Strava Routes offers a technology that selects a route optimized for the user-selected activity, such as running, horseback riding, walking, climbing, trail running, trekking, or mountain biking, and also bases the route on the user's current location. Instead of limiting itself to being an application that finds the fastest route, it provides the path and information most relevant to the user's current situation. For example, if the user is biking, they can use the service to find a route that avoids hills or follows a user-set preferred altitude, or choose between a paved or unpaved road depending on the sport. In addition, as the total length of the workout can be specified, the user is able to choose a route that fits the time of their workout and fully enjoy the activity without having to plan and match their time to the road situation.

Stage 2. Customization

The second stage of Proactive Technology is customization, which refers to when user-tailored functions can be automatically changed according to the context of the current situation. This dramatically increases user convenience.

IFTTT is an abbreviation for a conditional statement,

"If This, Then That", which means a predetermined action is performed when given a specific condition. For example, if the user is on vacation away from home for a long time, several automated actions can be set in advance, such as turning the lights on and off during certain times of the day, as well as immediately notifying the user if any movement is detected in the house. In addition to vacation mode, if the user chooses movie watching mode, sleep mode, away from home mode, etc., predefined functions are executed based on each of the conditional contexts. In addition, employees at a company that uses an open seating system can swipe their employee badge and have the height of the desk or monitor settings automatically changed to the last settings that they used – another example of stage two Proactive Technology.

Products equipped with the ability to automatically switch on and off certain functions based on the current environment of the user are also gradually catching on. The most widely found example is a TV or computer display adjusting its own brightness depending on the surrounding lighting settings. By adjusting the brightness and contrast of a device's backlight, or by judging whether a still image or a moving video is being displayed, the function helps save energy.

Recently, in facilities and apartments used by many people, windows with automatic ventilation systems are increasingly being installed. Kumho Petrochemical's Hugreen is a product in which automatic control technology comes with the window, while LX Hausys's automatic ventilation system and KT's AI clean ventilation systems are sensors that can be added to existing windows. These automatic ventilation windows check the atmospheric conditions outside the window such as smog, fine dust, pollen, and outdoor temperature, and on the inside detect temperature, humidity, and carbon dioxide concentrations. If the quality of indoor air is below a set standard, external air is let in automatically, and conversely, if the outdoor air is polluted, air purified by a filter is let into the room.

In the education industry, where learning speed and progress on homework assignments vary widely according to each student's academic level and problem-solving patterns, Proactive Technology is being used for customization. Woongjin ThinkBig's Smart All스마트올 provides customized tablet-based courses according to a student's level by analyzing their learning patterns and thought processes using AI. It gives each student a customized assignment to complete every day, gets down to the root cause of questions that they answered incorrectly, and repeats similar questions to encourage learning. In addition, if patterns such as skipping or guessing are detected when solving a problem, it gives real-time feedback discouraging the behavior. Because the courses and questions for each subject are constantly modified according to achievement level, different levels of highly customized teaching can be offered for each individual student even though they are all subscribed to the same single service.

Stage 3. Preemptive execution

The last stage of Proactive Technology is technology that predicts future events by identifying patterns and then taking preemptive action. If a person passes out due to excessive carbon dioxide exposure and the technology calls 911 after detecting the person's slumped or fallen posture, then that would be an example of stage two Proactive Technology using customization. However, if an abnormal concentration of carbon dioxide is detected indoors and the sensor recognizes that the person's facial expression, posture, and breathing patterns are different from usual, triggering an automatic window-opening function to ventilate the room, then the technology is an example of stage three Proactive Technology: preemptive execution.

Aeon Group, Japan's top shopping mall, was able to cut losses caused by disasters and thefts by 70% through its use of Proactive Technology to manage risk. Fujitsu's Human Sensing, introduced by Aeon Group at Aeon Style's Kawaguchi branch in May 2021, classifies individuals by gender and age, and utilizes images from existing surveillance cameras without collecting personal information. Even when a person is wearing a mask and has no detectable facial features, other information such as the person's posture is matched with movement data such as the person's gait, and the relationship to the people and objects in the person's proximity. Through this technology, when a person's behavior is considered suspicious enough to suggest a high probability of theft, a warning broadcast is sent out through the speaker. This technology is also applied in elderly care facilities. If a person's movements are different from usual, the technology detects and notifies the medical staff before an accident such as a fall occurs so that they can take quick action.

A field where preemptive action is most actively applied is autonomous driving. Advanced driver-assistance systems (ADAS) are representative examples of technology that has reached the level of preemptive action. These systems are crucial for autonomous vehicles as the technology recognizes numerous situations that occur while driving, makes a judgment of the situation, and then directly controls mechanical devices. The EU will make it mandatory for all new cars to be equipped with ADAS from 2024. Passenger monitoring technology is an ADAS function that checks the state of passengers using sensors mounted inside the car. The aim is to monitor the driver's heart rate, breathing, and stress level in real time, and to then send a signal so the driver or passengers can respond in advance.

At the archery event of the Tokyo 2020 Summer Olympic Games, Hyundai Motors supplied equipment that uses autonomous driving recognition technology, which detects minute color changes on the faces of players in competition to remotely measure pulse and heart rate. This technology, called a "vision-based heart rate measurement device," analyzes video of the athlete's face using frame-by-frame analysis to measure the athlete's level of tension or relaxation in real time. It is based on the principle that the color changes of people's faces reflect changes in heartbeat, and a separate facial recognition algorithm that deduces from facial expressions which player is about to shoot, while also filtering out ambient noise. For ADAS, this technology monitors driver's eyes and facial features, activating the autonomous driving function if it determines the driver to be distracted.

When Proactive Technology applied to automobiles meets smartphones, its predictive abilities are further enhanced. Samsung Electronics is developing a digital cockpit in partnership with Harman International, a global vehicle software company it acquired in 2016. By linking the car software with Samsung's health-tracking app on a smartphone, the driver's physical activities recorded on the smartphone (and any wearable device) prior to getting in the vehicle are periodically updated when the user gets in the car through this connected ecosystem of in-car monitoring devices, wearable devices, and smartphone. If the system determines through the user's current eyelid movement and sleep pattern of the previous night that the risk of drowsiness is high, it opens windows and increases ventilation while displaying a warning message to the driver. Depending on the driver's stress levels monitored by the system, automatic changes to the interior settings of the vehicle, such as lighting, fragrance, and music are made.

In real life, it is not yet easy to find products with technology that has reached this advanced stage. However, the underlying technology is developing rapidly, and implementation and mass adoption now just depends on the technology reaching a more advanced stage in understanding and preempting user behavior. For example, Eindhoven Airport, the second largest airport in the Netherlands by passenger traffic, aims to boost travelers' convenience by combining facial recognition technology with immigration control and a system that controls airport services such as shopping and dining. This system would not just offer basic functions such as notifying passengers of delayed flights through their smartphones, but would also suggest activities that users could try during their spare time. The latter is what would make the system an advanced form of Proactive Technology. The competitive edge for the future lies in which technology can first and most suitably determine users' needs and provide solutions to problems that have yet to occur.

Outlook and Implications

In August 2022, tragic news of the death of a mother and her two daughters in Suwon deeply saddened the public. The incident drew parallels to the 2014 "Songpa mothers and two daughters" tragedy, which shocked people in its revelations of loopholes in the Korean welfare system that had not been adequately improved. Welfare experts point out that the "Suwon mother and two daughters" case revealed the limits of the welfare system which is dependent on applicants taking action. The mother and daughters were in very poor health and did not apply for welfare despite their circumstances being so bad that they were unable to pay 17,000-won monthly health insurance premiums for 16 months. The media highlighted the unfortunate situation: if they had applied for welfare, they would have been able to receive about 1.25 million won a month. But as they had not updated their new address, authorities had not been aware of their situation.

This case underscored yet again the need for a "crisis household identification system" or "welfare that visits homes," which was called for after the "Songpa" incident, but it is also regrettable that the situation would have come to light sooner if the concept of Proactive Technology had been applied to public sector systems. If there had been an administrative network system that could link information such as electricity, water, and gas usage status, as well as overdue bill status of mobile phone bills and medical expenses, it would have facilitated welfare officials to reach out to them first, even if they did not apply for welfare payments or report moving to a new address.

Just as Proactive Technology can boost effectiveness in commercial settings, it can also maximize policy effectiveness when used in the public sector. For Proactive Technology in public services to work, localization must be of the utmost importance because the type of response required by users in each country or region varies widely. There is a growing need to apply Proactive Technology to national infrastructure in order to implement policies at a level that provides sufficient support for people's most basic needs.

Korea's public housing sector is also embracing proactive technologies. A representative example is the smart home service for public rental units that LH (Korea Land & Housing Corporation) plans to implement from the first half of 2023. In order to improve the level of support from the public rental housing network, a care system was introduced for people in need. This system, which can be controlled through smart devices, includes a combination of three levels of Proactive Technology. For senior residents, available services include automatically contacting the registered guardian when the resident's mobile phone has not been used for more than 12 hours, notifying the management office when an abnormality is detected by analyzing information such as the resident's location and water usage. In addition, social welfare services such as weather-tailored health information, health-related television programs, and medication timing reminders are also available. Technology is helping implement the goal of bringing public services closer to households.

Contrary to the existing paradigm, in which using technology was largely one-sided, Proactive Technology based on connected products which enables interactive communication for users is increasingly appealing to consumers, especially in the realm of smart homes. "Welcome to Raemian," mentioned earlier, is a prime example. "Smart home" refers to the implementation of functions that make life easier at home based on IoT technology, which uses AI to analyze living patterns and data of people in the home. This reflects how hyper-connected technologies have become more cost effective to the extent that they can now be used in daily life. However, this technology also has its drawbacks. All products purchased must be based on the same platform, or at least compatibility must be carefully checked whenever purchasing a new product.

Some companies, including Samsung Electronics, LG Electronics, Google, Amazon, and Apple, have adopted and developed an interoperability protocol called "Matter," providing an opportunity to bypass this inconvenience. This move reflects a shift in smart home-related technology to put the focus on the services rather than devices, which also reflects the fact that these customized and proactive services using AI are the end goal of the user experience rather than simple instances of automation. Going forward, the production process of products or services should start to move towards flexibly adjusting technology which actively analyzes and utilizes user data, and away from the current structure of production-side input. Synergies between consumers and technology will be maximized when technology can preemptively address potential problems and efficiently manage and handle these issues on its own while minimizing user inconveniences.

This trend that satisfies the minute needs of each individual user is already being commercialized, and the growing uptake can be seen in the choices consumers make. Consumers want businesses to be aware of how they can solve problems that arise during a product's use, rather than just at the purchase stage. Proactive technologies do not make consumers lazy. It should be the ultimate goal of technology to fulfill consumer needs by tracking changes in user behavior and preferences to preemptively avoiding problems.

In all technologies, the human aspect is key. The more technology advances, the closer it should move into people's everyday lives. Proactive Technology is bringing us one step closer to the end goal of technology.

Magic of
Real Spaces

What is the secret behind the spaces that customers have come to love? There is a power in Real Spaces that brings people together. This power can be divided into three types: (1) "gravitational force" that attracts people to a space; (2) "connectivity" that links with virtual spaces and enhances efficiency; and (3) "expandability" that broadens the horizon of a space through fusion with the metaverse. First, in order to create "gravitational force" that attracts people, the store should (a) either be made bigger to draw more customers, or smaller to be more centrally located and increase a chain's contact points; (b) offer a differentiated customer experience that customers can enjoy; and (c) provide a space that can be used as a forum for social interactions and exchanges among local residents. Second, in order to maximize the function of "connectivity," spaces should utilize data technologies and artificial intelligence to (a) provide customized services to customers; (b) help speed up the customer service at all stages between them and the product from the first mile to the last mile and everywhere in between; and (c) introduce the concept of "Retail-as-a-Service" (RaaS) to better analyze customers' in-store behavior. Finally, the "expandability" of a space must be considered in relation to facilitating connection to the metaverse. This means (a) users can feel the Real Space in the metaverse; (b) marketing activities that are seamlessly connected throughout the Real Space and the metaverse can be conducted; and (c) having a link between reality and the metaverse using virtual and augmented reality.

In order to take full advantage of new opportunities in this evolving world of space in the Covid-endemic era, companies and brands will have to offer – like a theme park – memorable and unique experiences.

"*A* time to reflect broadly and meditate deeply."

Since its open on November 12, 2021, there is a special exhibition hall with an average of 3,000 daily visitors. This place is the "Room of Quiet Contemplation" at the National Museum of Korea in Seoul. Among the young visitors, the space has become so hot that it has spawned the new term "Buddhist relaxation" and miniature statues of Buddha have completely sold out at the gift shop. And yet, in this room there are only two statues of Buddha on display. Why did these statues, which have been a part of the museum's permanent collection, provoke such an enthusiastic response? The answer lies in space. Visitors are first impressed by the unusually large space at 440 m². Then they are surprised by the completely different setting of the space compared to other exhibition rooms in the museum. There are no glass display cases and the statues can be viewed from all sides. This has transformed it into a space where everything – from the walls and floors, ceiling and Buddha statues, to even other visitors in the space – looks different from typical museum displays.

Spaces attract people, make them stay, and make them reflect. From the Chinese characters, "space空間" is a combination of the characters "empty空" and "between間," which literally means "empty space." But that empty space also leaves open the possibility that anything can happen, and objects can occupy the space. There are many more ways to read into space than just being "empty space."

Since the dawn of the internet, the concept of "virtual space" was born as an addition to the real-world space we live in. In this virtual space, it has become possible to perform functions comparable to what is possible in the real world, such as communicating and making transactions. Thus, the concept of "space" was divided into two types: online, or virtual space; and offline, or real-world space. Since then, as the capabilities and conveniences afforded from utilizing and communicating within virtual space have gained prominence with the development of technology, virtual space has even started to threaten real-world space in some sectors. With distribution chains in particular, the term "retail apocalypse" is appearing in the sense that retail channels based on traditional spaces are expected to lose competitiveness amid the rapid development of e-commerce. Moreover, this progression has intensified amid the pandemic's social distancing trend that has had a lingering effect on people's daily lives since 2020. Since then, many "brick-and-mortar" stores are facing challenges. From the massive department store chains that dominated the retail scene in the US and Japan to small neighborhood restaurants, stores are closing across the board. Is it really the end of physical spaces?

Not quite. Real Spaces still have an inherent power. While virtual space is typically divided into the online and offline realms, space in the real world cannot be simply confined to being the flipside of the online world. Real Space is the fundamental foundation and basis on which our lives unfold. It embodies a unique character and retains a powerful attractive force that has kept drawing people in even during the pandemic. Unremarkable spaces may fade away, but stores with their own character are constantly talked about and visited by people. What is the secret behind these spaces people have come to love? Also, during a time when alternative spaces online and in the metaverse are expanding rapidly, what kind of relationship should they have with Real Spaces to create synergies? We must think deeply about the power and the potential of these spaces.

In *Consumer Trend Insights 2023,* we focus on Real Spaces that bring people together by three types of power: (1) "gravitational force" that attracts and draws people to a space; (2) "connectivity" that links with virtual spaces and enhances efficiency; and (3) "expandability" that broadens the horizon of a space through fusion with the metaverse. Let's take a deeper look at these three types.

Gravitational Force: The Power to Attract People and Make them Stay

The gravitational force of a space is the power that attracts people and makes them stay, like the universal force of gravity. Real Space has its own set of advantages that cannot be replicated in virtual space. According to business administration professors Michael Levy and Barton Weitz, in a physical store customers are able to: (1) look and walk around; (2) experience "sensory shopping" where they can feel the physical properties of the product with their five senses; and (3) receive direct help from the store staff. However, as the growing trend of retail shows, online shopping has the powerful advantage of easy access and allows customers to compare a large number of products anytime and anywhere. Therefore, in order for physical space to compete and attract customers amid this industry shift, diverse and creative strategies need to be explored.

Bigger and closer

Physical space has the power to attract people. Among the theories regarding location in retail, the gravity model explains this well. The Huff Gravity Model is based on Newton's law of universal gravitation that all masses attract one another with a gravitational force proportional to their masses and inversely proportional to the square of the distance between them. Following this, the Huff Gravity Model claims that larger stores attract more customers, and the farther away the stores are from shopping centers, the less attractive they become.

The theory of gravitational force in terms of physical spaces implies that store size is the primary factor in attractiveness to customers. This model can also explain why "big-box" stores, which are large-scale distribution stores such as shopping malls and department stores, are highly capable of attracting customers. It's the same reason why stores in the same retail category that complement one another and are clustered together (e.g., a furniture district or a fashion street) exert a stronger gravitational pull on customers than stand-alone stores. This is also called the principle of "cumulative attraction": a cluster forms, increasing the collective size of the whole store and enhancing the effect of the gravitational force.

After the pandemic, the reopening of retail is underway with local retail groups unveiling large-scale investment and construction plans by building large stores. Lotte Group plans to renovate its main stores and build large complex malls, while the Shinsegae Group plans to open new Starfield shopping complexes in Suwon, Changwon, and Cheongna (Incheon), as well as allocating a larger budget for its Hwasung theme park and complex development projects. In 2022, large-scale theme parks such as Lotte World

Busan and Legoland have opened. As with online markets, the construction of large infrastructure projects is expected to play a significant role in driving the direction of physical retail store trends.

Another way to fully utilize the gravitational force of attracting customers is to shorten the distance between them and stores. Contrary to the big-box strategy, this method consists of developing many small stores which are located closer to customers. Amazon is preparing to open a 30,000 m² department store, which is around one-third the size of a typical department store. Through this store size reduction strategy, it plans to increase flexibility and expand points of contact with its customers. This strategy and moving stores into the city center are important distribution trends. Nordstrom Local is a smaller "service hub" version of the American department store chain, which has moved towards increasing points of contact with its customers. IKEA, which has traditionally pursued a large-scale store strategy, has also opened a small store in Manhattan and will continue to open small stores in city centers. In Japan, it has also opened small experimental stores such as IKEA Planning Studio and IKEA Lab. The strategy is to increase the gravitational force by closing the physical distance that lies between physical stores and their customers.

While a store's format – large or small – will set the strategic direction that strengthens its gravitational force, a dualized strategy that can combine the advantages of large and small stores will increasingly emerge as a trend of physical retail stores.

Creating customer experience

A book cafe called "Cafe Comma" can be found on the first and second floors of the Shinyoung Securities Building in the Yeouido district of Seoul. It is always packed with fans of books and coffee lovers alike. The space used to be a large bookstore but closed down due to slow business. In theory, large bookstores would seem much more efficient in selling books given their larger space to display and carry books. However, the book cafe, which uses that same large space, has performed better. Why? Customer experience holds the key. By purchasing a cup of coffee, customers can choose from 15,000 books in a 1,650 m² space and spend all day reading. Even if the space is utilized in a somewhat less efficient way, it needs to be competitive by providing a customer experience that cannot be experienced anywhere else. This example shows why the commercial space is moving hand in hand with the food, coffee, and dessert markets.

What should the key attributes of customer experience in physical stores be? Authors Joseph Pine and James Gilmour state the importance of the "experience economy" and emphasize that creating experiences is what differentiates businesses amid the flood of goods and services. In the experience economy, consumers go beyond the concept of simple users or clients and must be treated with sincerity as guests. The seller must become a production director, provide memorable experiences that go beyond functional transactions, and create sensations for customers.

An example of an implementation of this experience economy model are the Showfields stores in the United States. As the name suggests, Showfields is a place that puts on a show. Customers make reservations in advance and upon entering the store are introduced to various products in the form of a performance. A brand becomes the theme of the show at Showfields. Actors perform to demonstrate the products while customers interact with one another. After the performance, they can purchase products as they

⟨ Characteristics of the Experience Economy ⟩

	Commodities	Services	Experiences
Economic Function	Extract	Deliver	Stage
Nature of Offering	Fungible	Intangible	Memorable
Seller	Trader	Provider	Stager
Buyer	Market	Client	Guest
Factors of Demand	Characteristics	Benefits	Sensations

Source: Joseph Pine and James Gilmore (2011), *The Experience Economy*, Updated Edition

would souvenirs after enjoying a day at a theme park.

There is a comparable experience in Korea in which customer experience is amplified through this type of performance. "Jeju Haenyeo's Kitchen제주 해녀의 부엌" in Jeju Island has converted an old, abandoned fish market by the pier into a performance hall and restaurant. A play about the lives of *haenyeo* (the female divers of Jeju) is performed for guests who have booked in advance, and real *haenyeo* make an appearance to tell their story. After watching the performance, guests can enjoy an elaborate full-course meal. Using original content related to Jeju Island and the lives of *haenyeo* and seafood as the subject, it offers consumers a local experience that cannot be experienced anywhere else. This is an example of how the value and depth of experience can improve when performance is an added dimension to customer experience.

To maximize customer experience, even the most minute details of the visit need to be carefully planned. Customers may think that they are just walking down an ordinary hallway in a large shopping space, but in most cases they are following a route planned by space planning experts that have chosen that layout after careful consideration. This is called "promenade retail," and it is also referred to as a "retail conveyor belt" because customers shop as if they were traveling along a moving sidewalk. For example, the commercial promenade concept of The Hyundai Seoul is based on street culture, which is one of the new cultural codes of Generation MZ. Even luxury goods are adding aspects of street culture through various collaborations, making it more mainstream. That culture is replicated in the retail stores of The Hyundai Seoul to make the customer experience more interesting.

A space for sharing and social exchange

Modern commercial space is also used as a venue for social exchange. It has developed into a space where people with similar tastes gather and connect. Spaces that brands operate becomes a place of social exchange by providing a customer experience that attracts people with similar tastes. This helps create a relationship with the brand through active participation in the experience. In an increasingly fragmented and atomized society, providing a means of strengthening connection through exchanges are becoming important functions of these spaces.

Nobuo Tomae, president of MUJI's planning division, defines offline stores as a type of "community infrastructure where people connect." The function of brick-and-mortar stores, which are gradually disappearing, is not limited to just selling products. When MUJI opens new stores, it offers differentiated services by localizing and including regional characteristics in the stores. MUJI considered its physical stores a type of "community center."

For effective social exchange, the space should be planned and designed in such a way that it reflects the characteristics of the local community and enables connection and cooperation with local residents. Ace Hotel, which began in Portland, Oregon and has 13 branches around the world, is based on this philosophy. From the 1990s, undervalued historical buildings were selected and through collaboration with local creators designed a unique hotel, and a local platform was created by signing up small local businesses to offer their services in the hotel. The hotel actively collaborates with local brands and provides spaces to guests as well as local residents.

A hostel called "Okrim Inn옥림여관" in Jeju is also specialized in this form of providing a forum for local socializing. It connects guests with nearby bicycle shops to make it easier for travelers to get around, and it collaborates with local fitness clubs to provide gym services for guests. In addition, events such as movie screenings are held so that nearby residents can visit the hostel without having to stay a night there. The Shibuya Trunk Hotel in Japan also serves as a central community center for the area. Local artists and creators hold exhibitions, all items sold at the hotel store are local products, and all food served at the restaurant is locally sourced. The hotel refers to itself as a socializing platform and prioritizes the local community.

Connectivity: The Power Connecting Virtual and Real Spaces

Online and Real Spaces no longer exist independently of each other. They complement each other, and in many cases Real Spaces have become more convenient by utilizing digital technology. While preserving the advantages of Real Spaces, various solutions that enable a connected and digital experience in the physical space are unfolding. Through the expansion of an "on-off blending" strategy of the physical and the digital, customers using physical stores stand to benefit.

Tailored to the individual

Personalized recommendation services which are made possible through artificial intelligence and big data analysis in online transactions are now essential. Now, even in offline space, such technology is combined to offer a new level of personalized services. McDonald's, for example, has replaced the traditional menu with a smart menu display that changes menu items in real time by combining data according to the weather, time of day, and order status at the store using AI. For example, during lunchtime in the summer, carbonated beverages such as Coke, rather than coffee, are displayed in the front. AI recognizes the license plate of the car entering the drive-thru, brings up the customer's previous order, and the menu changes automatically to a customized version. It is a data-driven strategy that maximizes customer response rates in physical stores.

The world's first brick-and-mortar fashion store from Amazon, the Amazon Style store, which opened in Los Angeles in May 2022, utilizes cutting-edge technologies such as big data, AI, machine learning, and logistics networks. Instead of simply displaying piles of clothes in the store, there is a space where clothing is displayed in the most flattering combination. When customers scan the QR code attached to the clothing hanger, the Amazon shopping app shows the price, color, size, and customer reviews of the product on their smartphone as if they were shopping online. In addition, AI recommends other clothes tailored to the customer's interests. Once the shopper has decided on the clothes they want, they press a button in the app that signals the selected clothes to be brought to the fitting room by the store staff. A touchscreen display on one side of the fitting room shows a list of other products recommended by AI, and any additional clothes that are chosen there can be delivered to the shopper to try on without leaving the fitting room.

Through this method, Amazon-style fitting rooms do not require customers to pick up their own clothes from the racks or go through the trouble of going out to get a different size. Amazon-style stores use physical space and digital technology to overcome the limitations of online purchases and maximize the advantages of physical stores through technology. This shopping platform goes beyond a simple shopping experience where you can see and buy clothes to give users easy access to information on their clothing choices as well as to offer new shopping experiences. Amazon refers to this approach as "reinventing in-store shopping."

Logistics speed going the 'extra mile'

The main advantage of a physical store is instant gratification. Buyers don't have to wait for the product to be delivered as they can just pick up what they want and leave. Humans have the psychological tendency of wanting to minimize the time between wanting something and getting it. Physical stores satisfy this desire, so they have a significant edge in terms of convenience compared to shopping online. Yet, in order to maximize these advantages of physical stores, digital technology is crucial. For example, in the case of US retail chains Kroger and Target, customers visiting a store can create a shopping list on an app so they can be efficiently guided through and to the sections they need. Lowe's uses its NAVii robot to help customers find the products they need. By incorporating technology into physical stores, convenience and speed improves.

Then there are cases in which not only the speed of buying products improves but also the speed of returns. In a report on the future of stores after the pandemic, global real estate and investment firm CBRE notes not only the changes being made to the display racks in the store, but also to the returns section. Customers can return both online and offline purchases in the store. When they do, providing a return space in a highly visible place within the store is seen as playing an important role in improving customer experience. Customers are also more likely to come back and shop again in the store. For this reason, Walmart and Best Buy are also expanding the return areas in their stores.

Department store retail chain Kohl's has been operating an Amazon return center since 2019 and is using it as a channel to draw Amazon customers to Kohl's stores. It is notable that the return space is an important factor in enhancing the complete service of the physical store and improving customer experience. As such, it is now necessary to carefully consider the extra mile in addition to the first mile, middle mile, and last mile in logistics. Here, the "extra mile" refers to the additional service that occurs in the form of returns due to customers changing their minds or other reasons after completing the journey from the first to the last mile.

Offline stores analyzing customer behavior

Offline stores are a great opportunity to analyze customer behavior. Companies that actively use this as one of their business models are emerging. A representative example is "b8ta," which drew a lot of attention after closing a physical store and displaying the message "our experiment was successful." The company is a service retailer with a chain of over 20 standalone retail stores that does not focus primarily on selling merchandise. By fitting out the stores' floor space with the latest technologies, they are used as a type of presentation center.

Brands that want to sell their products in the store rent out a space through a subscription agreement with b8ta. In the stores, multiple cameras are installed on the ceiling to analyze the behavior of customers. The cameras collect data for each product, such as the amount of time customers stand in front of a particular shelf, the number of customers who just pass by the shelf, or how much time the clerk spends giving explanations or demonstrations to customers for the product. In addition to these data points, it collects customer-specific data and sends demographic information such as age and gender of customers interested in the product to the companies that rented out b8ta's space. After analyzing this data with AI, companies can use it for sales and new product development or planning.

Blank, an experiential shopping store in Germany, operates a store to analyze customer behavior similar to b8ta. This store also monitors customer movement and analyzes shopping cart data using AI. Tsutaya Home Appliances in Japan also runs a similar store that collects customer behavior data in the store using an AI camera. It has positioned itself as an offline data media platform by measuring the real-time reaction of customers in front of branded products in stores that cannot be measured online and then provides the analyzed data to store brands that rent space in the store.

In September 2019, consulting firm McKinsey opened an offline store called Modern Retail Collective in Minnesota. A variety of products such as jewelry, cosmetics, and clothing are available for sale there. It was used as a retail lab where customers were able to experience new brands and retail technology. In the store, collecting data on each customer's behavior, and using chatbots to gain sophisticated insights into the consumer experience, such as the reason for the customer's purchase (or the reason for not making a purchase), can all be used to improve the shopping experience. McKinsey calls this type of distribution "Retail-as-a-Service (RaaS)."

Expandability: The Power of Space Applied to the Metaverse

Recently, the concept of space has been expanding beyond the simple dichotomy of the online and real worlds to include a third space, the "metaverse," which is a reflection of the real world. The most basic way to expand real-world spatial experience to the metaverse is to set up a store in virtual reality so that users can experience a comparable version of the offline store. For example, Hyundai Department Store opened "VR Pangyo Land," a virtual department store where you can have a 360-degree look around the store with your mobile phone. This virtual place gives the feeling as if you are walking through a real department store by capturing the space on a mobile platform. Viewers can look around in the store through VR and catch up on information on events being held in the department store.

For some stores which have set up VR showrooms, viewers can take a closer look at the products displayed in the store, purchase the product they want through the connected online shopping mall, or make the purchase directly with the store staff through KakaoTalk. Also, mini games are available at intervals along the virtual space to make the experience more enjoyable and customers are also able to enjoy VR exhibitions such as art museums and AR photo zones when they want to take a break from shopping.

Marketing strategies which link Real Spaces to the metaverse can create significant synergy. A prime example is Chipotle, a Mexican restaurant chain in the United States. Chipotle opened a virtual restaurant inside Roblox for Halloween. When the avatar visits the store, an employee in the shape of a skull invites customers to choose from a variety of Halloween costumes to change into. When customers enter wearing Halloween costumes and strike up a conversation with the staff, Chipotle offers free burrito coupons on a first come, first served basis. This event was notable in that the brand was able to extend their metaverse experience into the real world by issuing coupons that can be used in actual Chipotle restaurants, and on their website and app. For years, Chipotle held annual Halloween events where customers who wore Halloween costumes and visited stores nationwide received discounts on food; now this tradition has been extended to the metaverse.

With multiple brands across fashion, music, and sports sectors entering the metaverse, McDonald's has applied for trademarks for virtual food and beverage products, downloadable multimedia files including artwork, text, audio and video files, and NFTs, which are expected to be part of its push to sell food in the virtual world. McDonald's is currently preparing several virtual events, including virtual concerts, and is also planning a virtual restaurant that handles both real food and virtual food at the same time. In the case of real food ordered within the metaverse, it will be provided through a delivery service.

Moreover, there are attempts to create a parallel space of the real-world space in the metaverse called a "digital twin" for the purpose of analyzing and improving the Real Space. Microsoft's Dynamics 365 is a product that helps analyze sales maximization or marketing effects by recreating a physical store into a digital space for experimental purposes. Through the use of cameras installed in the store, the internal structure of the store and the movement of customers are identified, replicated, and visualized in the digital space. This allows deeper analysis of customer behavior. It uses cameras that point to the entrance and exit to track store visits and monitor which times of the day or the week are trending. Users can even identify the busiest days of the week and use the data to manage wait times. Users can also measure how long customers wait in queues and use the data to manage queues and cashiers. It is also possible to analyze peak hours of customer visits, the duration of their stays, and which products are looked at longest.

By using these solutions, companies can analyze how products should be placed and displayed, and how to operate stores to increase customer stay time or visit rates. It is a method of moving real data over to the digital, devising an optimal marketing method, and applying it to reality.

As economic activity in virtual markets based on the creator economy is rapidly expanding, retailers are facing changes in which they need to interpret and adapt the customer experience provided in the Real Space to the virtual space. In the future, companies will be able to enhance the customer experience and make it more immersive by offering so-called "meta-commerce" services connected with the virtual economy and improving the Real Space using digital twin technology.

Outlook and Implications

The pandemic has shrunk the need for Real Spaces yet at the same time has made people want more real-world activities and experiences. This phenomenon is evident in consumer trends in the real world. Online activity may be efficient and convenient, but the sensory experience of the real world can never be replicated. Now, the priority is focusing on how to make sure Real Spaces shift from just retail distribution to a medium to attract, communicate with, and inform people. What are the new functions of Real Spaces following the pandemic and in what direction should companies go to take full advantage of the power of space?

A space is not simply a place for retail distribution. It is an effective form of media that can add value. As a company would plan a campaign with advertisements or promotional media, they can also utilize their store space for marketing activities. A good example is Gentle Monster. As of 2021, Gentle Monster, which is valued at 1 trillion won and has set up over 400 stores in 30 countries around the world, does not advertise through traditional media. Instead, they have developed a strategy to deliver their brand message by making store spaces their channel. That is one of the most important roles of Real Spaces for brands. Gentle Monster has grown its brand value through spatial marketing. Viral marketing that stems from these stores encourage consumers to help spread brand awareness.

D2C (direct-to-consumer) commerce brands are also following the offline store trend. Musinsa, which sells fashion products, Warby Parker, a brand that sells glasses, and Everlane, a fashion brand famous for its transparent pricing policy, have all opened brick-and-mortar stores. The primary purpose of these stores is not sales. Instead, they function as a type of media channel to promote brand awareness and communicate with customers. This is because marketing stemming from these physical spaces can be more cost effective than marketing through paid media.

CEO Choi Won-seok, who created pop-up store platform business "Project Rent" said, "I want to create a space in the form of a magazine which showcases individuals and brands with good content." Moving away from the stereotype that only large corporations can open pop-up stores, there are more opportunities to market small- and medium-sized brands through these channels. That has led to the trend of brands using a physical space to market their brands to consumers and introduce new products for a limited period of time instead of renting out stores for an extended period. It's not about selling products but about creating a space filled with content to promote the brand.

The real space has the advantage of offering customers the closer experience of seeing and touching the brand's products. The influence that spaces can have in marketing can be more powerful than any other medium.

The conclusion is customers

"Be our guest!"

This is a song sung by candlesticks, bowls, and teacups in Disney's animated film *Beauty and the Beast.* More than just a song in a movie, it can be seen as Disney's slogan that exemplifies space management at Disneyland. Disney has its own "guestology" formula to enhance customer experience. Organizing and delivering services from the customer's point of view, as one would treat a guest that has visited one's home, is key. Breaking down each stage of service during a person's stay at Disneyland and creating a refined, personalized experience at each stage is the core strategy. Disney is known for training each of its employees to act as if they are a magician that leads customers into fantasy worlds. In particular, they make each customer feel special through personalized attention.

To carry out this strategy, Disney offers ways for guests to immerse themselves in the experience using all five senses, creating the illusion of a fantasy world. They do their best to provide services that exceed customers' expectations. From first-class face-to-face customer service to analyzing the customer experience from the visitor's point of view, the focus is on how to better use infrastructure design and customer interactions to provide a great experience.

These are not just strategies that apply to theme parks like Disneyland. They are common in retail distribution spaces. A theme park like Disneyland and a department store have a lot in common. Both spaces are spacious landmarks that provide fun and entertainment to people. They hold festivals and the employees are welcoming. Through various methods they both create fantasy worlds for a momentary escape from reality. Commercial spaces should have the characteristics of theme parks that provide the best customer experience imaginable.

Jacques Lacan described everyday life as a boring passageway to death and emphasized that the extraordinary and what provides a sense of fantasy is what can break that monotony. The ability of space to survive the decline of physical retail spaces after the pandemic will rely on successfully creating new spaces through extraordinary themes and concepts. As virtual worlds grow, for Real Space to retain its own power, its starting point and end goal must be the customer.

Peter Pan
and

the Neverland
Syndrome

Looking and living younger than a person's actual age have become virtues in Korean society. Like Peter Pan and his friends living forever as children in Neverland, we would like to call the trend of Peter Pans who refuse to age "Neverland Syndrome." Neverland Syndrome can be classified into three different types. (1) Those who want to go back to childhood by purchasing items such as princess toy sets or Pokémon pastries; (2) those who try not to age, not just by maintaining a youthful appearance, but by going as far as declining promotions at work; and (3) those who are obsessed with having fun and who cheerfully pursue – like children – easy and fun activities. The spread of this trend signals an increase in people searching for comfort from nostalgia for childhood as they face an increasingly challenging and uncertain future. But the most fundamental cause lies in structural changes in people's life cycles as a direct result of longer human lifespans. The period that constitutes one's youth has lengthened as people live longer. As they live longer, their life stages diversify, leading to the disappearance of previous stereotypes of what the life of a "typical" adult figure should look like. Neverland Syndrome also raises concerns about the side effects of society moving towards more infantile personalities. Self-centered behaviors, obsessing over inanimate objects, blaming others or the government for personal problems, and being preoccupied with their own tastes and preferences are all related to typically childish behavior.

How do we maximize the high-energy, positive aspects of youth while minimizing the immature ones? Whether Neverland will turn out to be a utopia or a dystopia depends on society's collective efforts to address this question. When we can embrace the positive aspects of youth rather than its infantile and irresponsible egocentrism, we as a society will get closer to reaching true maturity.

Recently, the number of so-called "kidults" has been on the rise. A middle-aged man carrying a cell phone in a red Iron Man case; a middle-aged woman wearing Hello Kitty accessories; a senior citizen who is proud to declare herself a fan of young singer Lim Young-woong. With people wearing masks these days, it is not uncommon to find instances where it is difficult to tell whether the two people walking by are a mother and daughter, sisters, or a grandmother and granddaughter from looking at their attire alone. More and more people are calling themselves "kidults" because they feel they don't fit the stereotype of what they had previously thought constitutes "being an adult."

In Korean society, living younger than one's actual age is becoming a virtue. "You look so young" is considered a much bigger compliment than "you look great." Kidults, who obsess over collecting children's toys, had until now been regarded as a minority group of extreme fans with far from mainstream tastes. The perception of kidults has since been changing, shifting more towards awe and admiration. Now, adults do not confine themselves to fit within the traditional stereotype of how adults should look or act, but value pursuing happiness in their own way. Some express this by obsessing over any and all things cute, making claims such as, "cute things will come to save the world," while others seek fun in everyday life by acting childishly. People think of their present selves as an extension of their childhood and look to their childhood to help them find the key to understanding their complicated inner selves.

In the play *Peter Pan; or, the Boy Who Wouldn't Grow Up* by British author J. M. Barrie, Peter Pan lives in "Neverland" and never ages, staying forever a child. In pop-psychology, "Peter Pan syndrome" refers to a degenerative psychological state in which a person attempts to remain, psychologically, a child in an adult body. Neverland is a place where other children – the Lost Boys – join Peter and enjoy adventures together, and they too do not age. Global pop star Michael Jackson named his mansion the "Neverland Ranch" which was styled like a theme park with the goal being he could relive his lost childhood and never grew old. At that time, people thought of Jackson as eccentric, and that the Neverland Ranch was something only a rich celebrity could pull off. But today, the desire to live like a child without getting old has become much more common. In other words, staying young in Korean society is not just a preference of the few but is becoming a way of thinking and even a *modus vivendi* for society as a whole. The pursuit of youth has reached the stage of obsession beyond an object of admiration and affection.

We would like to call the trend of these Peter Pans who refuse to age "Neverland Syndrome," after Peter Pan's magical island home. While Peter Pan syndrome refers to a maladaptive state in which a person regresses to being a child and isolating themselves from the adult world, "Neverland Syndrome" is a neutral term that refers to the trend in which many people consider themselves younger than their actual age and enjoy calling themselves "kidults." Let's take a look at how Neverland Syndrome manifests itself in all parts of Korean society. We will also look into the background of this youth-seeking phenomenon and what implications it holds for society.

The Three Types of Neverland Syndromes

Neverland Syndrome can be divided into three categories. The first is those who want to return to their childhood; the second is those who want to stay in their present state and not get any older; and the third is those who want to play like children and have fun.

1. Return: Back to childhood

Fashion accessories of celebrities such as Han So-hee and

Tae-yeon recently became a hot topic. One of them was an accessory set called the "Princess Necklace Set" consisting of pink earrings and necklaces with considerably large jewels. It is not a luxury brand product but a plastic toy accessory for children priced between 1,000 and 3,000 won. Toy "princess sets" have recently emerged as fashionable items. Since then, people of all ages, from children to middle-aged, have been posting photos of themselves wearing princess accessory sets on social media, even leading to a shortage of the product. Childish glamour has gone from being awkward to trendy, allowing people to shine and be the center of attention.

But this childhood kitsch is not limited to princess accessories for a casual dinner party. An eye-catching, all-pink store has opened in Hannam-dong, an area that is lined with stylish and modern restaurants and cafés. As its name, "Royal Melting Club," suggests, this dessert café is a space that has become the "it" place for the country's "pink princesses," with all manner of sparkling decorations adorning the store's interior, chairs, and tables, as well as merchandise. The café also offers services for children, such as a kid's baking class, but most of the customers who visit this place are adults who are looking for its signature cake with a tiara or a colorful cartoon character dessert. Many of them are female consumers who just love anything pink. Breaking the unwritten rule that children play spaces and adult hangouts are separate places, here the tastes of both adults and children have merged into one.

Pokémon Bread, which sold out nationwide in March 2022, is an example of just how many kidults are out there. This product, which had been popular among children in the 1990s, made a nostalgia-inducing comeback. It was a hit for everyone, from teenagers to forty-somethings, bringing back childhood memories for adults that could be shared as something fun and new with today's teenagers. Pokémon Bread sold 10 million units within 43 days of its release, far exceeding the popularity it enjoyed in the 1990s. This is where we can see youthful taste now becoming mainstream and no longer being limited to just a few fanatics.

Kidults going mainstream is not unique to Korea. The US toy industry also considers kidults to be a consumer group warranting close attention in the future. Global toy manufacturer Lego launched a marketing campaign called "Adults Welcome" in the United States in 2020, creating a separate section for adults on its homepage. In addition, American trade association The Toy Association, which annually selects a "Product of the Year", established a new award in 2022: "Adult Toy of the Year." 58% of American adult respondents said they had bought a toy or board game for themselves, according to the association's 2021 survey.

2. Stay: Refusing to age

The 2022 blockbuster movie that filled long-vacant cinemas after two years of the pandemic was *Top Gun: Maverick*. As with most blockbusters, the production quality was high, but what was talked about most was the charm that actor Tom Cruise still possessed and that had changed little since his appearance in the first installment in 1986, over 30 years ago. His physique at his age is the definition of "never growing old." Of particular note was that Maverick, the role played by Tom Cruise, never achieved the flag rank of admiral and performed his test pilot duties as a captain. Iceman, who appeared as a rival colleague in the previous movie, died of cancer after being promoted to commander of the Pacific Fleet, while Maverick continued to carry out daily operations. The line, "It's not the plane. It's the pilot," lit a fire in the hearts of the middle-aged audience, some of whom may have felt they have become obsolete, like the retired F-14 fighter jet. The audience focused on Iceman and Maverick's different life paths: between a life of reaching a top rank, but dying prematurely, and a life of never getting promoted, but still as active as ever, who of the two is more admired?

In Korean society, where seniority culture has deep roots, growing old meant that an employee would be promoted in the organization, from a worker to a manager, and later to a decision maker, in a predictable sequence up the corporate ladder. However, more people have now started to think that being promoted does not necessarily need to be a natural progression of a career. Although promotions come with the benefit of more authority, increased wages, and social recognition, they also come with more responsibilities and, in some cases, employment instability. So, rather than giving up their work-life balance by getting promoted, some hope to stay in their position for as long as they can. In addition, there is a changing mindset that the workers are not in a subordinate relationship with their managers, but that the two positions just reflect two different jobs with different characteristics. This has much to do with companies introducing a remuneration system in which they pay corresponding compensation for the jobs each employee is responsible for. In the past, a manager returning to an ordinary employee position was considered degrading and humiliating because the move to a managerial position was always seen as a promotion.

Fandom culture among seniors has also drawn attention for being just as enthusiastic as fandom among younger age groups. An academy specializing in fandom has been established to support fans who start their fan activities at a later age. Free courses run by singer Lim Young-woong's fans teach latecomer fans about how to sign up to music sites, as well as the different ways to support their favorite celebrity.

In Korean society, aging had once been synonymous with growth. As people got older, their appearance changed, their rank in organizations rose, and their relationships and tastes matured. In other words, there was a set sequence to follow that was appropriate for a person at a certain age. But recently, this formula has been losing ground. More and more people don't want to change, whether it be maturity level or age. Take appearance: youthful looks are considered more valuable than old ones. Among celebrities and the people who are interested in their appearance, it has always been a priority to look young. But when it comes to experts and professionals across various fields, looking older had typically been preferred. That was because older looks had been a symbol of having a lot of experience, which in turn implied the person was skilled at their profession. However, as more people in their 30s are being promoted to executives of large corporations, there is no longer a direct link between skills and age. Now, youthful appearance is seen as a measure of self-care and discipline. Someone giving a compliment by saying "I can't tell how old you are" means that that person has taken great care of themselves. As such, youth offers a competitive edge.

3. Play: Having fun like a child

"I don't know when I'll actually be able to play golf well, but all I want is to just have fun with people I like."

#MyeongrangGolf #Golfkids #Golfstagram

After the pandemic, more "golf kids" have started playing golf, and on social media there is one hashtag that appears frequently. The hashtag is "MyeongrangGolf명랑골프," which as of September 2022 featured on over 520,000 Instagram posts. Literally translated as "cheerful golf," it refers to a golf game that people can enjoy comfortably with friends and without strictly following the rules or focusing on the score. Golf is a sport with complicated and strict rules that go as far to classify the qualifications of referees. Players themselves must also strictly abide by the rules. It is a game where improving one's skills takes a lot of practice. So, it is crucial for players to be very serious about the sport and to be fully immersed in the game to really enjoy it. The expression "dedicated golfer" says it all. Yet the reason golf has suddenly become a light and "cheerful" activity is due to the pandemic. Golf culture has changed dramatically as young people looking for social activities that can be enjoyed outdoors have turned to golf. They prioritize fun and play golf as a hobby, rather than focusing on the seriousness of the game as a sport.

"Fun" is a concept most associated with children. Children's cartoons are made to be entertaining and cheerful and are generally easy and enjoyable variations of adult cartoons. The third characteristic of Neverland Syndrome is that anything that falls under the category *"umgeunjin*엄근진*"*(an abbreviated term of the Korean words "strict엄격," "solemn근엄," and "serious^{진지}") is converted into a fun and cute version as though it were seen through the cheerful filter of a cartoon.

In Neverland, even the most complicated things can be easily accepted. In other words, even difficult subjects are softened. Originally, "softening" was a term used in the media. The softening of news refers to the fact that while most news stories cover "hard news," the majority of news consumption is centered on "soft news" – entertainment and human-interest stories – rather than news of urgent and public importance. However, there has recently been a trend where we see softening of content in general. Not only has the subject matter that is consumed become much lighter, but the form, style, and difficulty of the content are softened to make them easier for consumers to understand. Representative examples are the growth in popularity of "three-minute summaries" produced for easy consumption. This trend can be seen in the widely available "card news" type of summarized news content that conveys media reports in short sentences on a couple of slides, rather than in full paragraphs. "Picture journals그림일기," which are frequently found on social media these days, are one example of content softening. Among "Instatoons" (web cartoons serialized on Instagram), there are many "everyday toons" that express daily life or simple short stories in ten pictures or less. These everyday toons transform an essay into a picture journal that doesn't rely on a well-formed, compelling storyline with an intricate plot, but focuses instead on entertaining moments in daily life. At times, these toons point out the awkward social interactions or uncomfortable truths they encounter in daily life and serve as a means of delivering messages that may otherwise be too heavy or serious subject matters for readers.

Another way to have fun is to make daily life more entertaining. The recently popular "No Spending Challenge" is a prime example of injecting something playful into daily life. It describes a trend on social media to accept the challenge of reducing daily expenses to zero by, say, walking instead of taking the bus or a taxi, or packing a lunch box instead of eating out, which is essentially no different from how consumers have been saving cash in previous economic downturns. However, the difference is that the process is now being approached as one would playing a game, like a player who completes a quest in a video game, rather than a desperate act of saving up in the face of the harsh economic reality. These challenges also exemplify how playful characteristics can increase the entertainment value of an activity done in a group rather than on one's one.

The most important point to pay attention to in Neverland is the "character" trend. Cute and funny characters are popping up everywhere. A typical example is the giant rubber duck that appeared in Seokchon Lake in Jamsil, Seoul in 2014. Both adults and children were enthusiastic about the bath toy's unexpected and bigger-than-life appearance.

About 5 million people visited Seokchon Lake in the span of a month to see the giant duck. Based on the past history of its popularity, Lotte World Tower hosted the "Rubber Duck Project Seoul 2022" in October 2022. Kakao Friends characters Ryan and Choonshik, who have become national characters, are so popular they even formed a dance group. Other popular characters such as Lotte Home Shopping's bear character Bellygom벨리곰 and Hyundai Department Store's Willy have played important roles as brand ambassadors. These characters have become celebrities.

There's also a link between these characters and actual spending. Hite Jinro's "Jinro Is Back" ad campaign, whose mascot came to be called "toad soju," is an example where the brand broke tradition. Historically, soju advertisements featured the hottest female entertainers at the time. But now, a cute toad character took on that role in the brand's advertisements. Sales of the product increased by 37% in 2021. Thanks to the popularity, Hite Jinro operated pop-up stores that sold toad character merchandise around the country, like a pop star on a nationwide tour. This love for characters by adults is also apparent in the numbers. In a survey conducted by the Korea Creative Content Agency in 2021, 62.4% of the respondents said that the character influenced their decision when purchasing a product, and 53% said they were willing to pay more for character merchandise. The local character market is expected to grow from 2.7 trillion won in 2005 to 20 trillion won in 2022.

Background and Concerns

"Youth: all of us, or at least most, want to be honorary citizens of that country that we lost long ago. 'I still feel young,' say people in their forties, fifties and even sixties, and they may be right in their childish revolt against the obvious."

This is from Pascal Bruckner's *A Brief Eternity: The Philosophy of Longevity*, according to whom youth in the past was an obstacle to success. But now, people strive for youth and want to stay in that world. *The Curious Case of Benjamin Button*, who is born old, ages in reverse, and dies as an infant, has become the dream of modern people. Why is that?

Why society is getting younger

There are several ways to interpret the characteristics of Neverland. One is that people find comfort in childhood nostalgia when faced with a difficult and uncertain future, and another is that the demand for toys has grown across all age groups due to isolating at home during the pandemic. As explained in Chapter 6 on "Digging Momentum," it may also just be someone's way of finding happiness through immersion in a hobby that brings back good memories.

A much more fundamental factor lies in the background of the youth-seeking trend: people are living longer. As lifespans change, human life cycles are also undergoing structural changes. It is said that the human lifespan 100 years ago was about 500,000 hours, but the lifespan of a person today is about 700,000 hours. When expressed as a 24-hour period, when the average lifespan was 60 years, age 40 is already 4:00 p.m.; but when the average lifespan is 80 years, 40 is only noon. When a lifespan reaches 100 years, noon is, of course, 50 years of age. This additional time humans have today means people view aging as an extension of adolescence rather than moving into old age. Life, which had followed a binary structure of being young and then growing old, is being redefined in the 21st century as having several stages and transition periods before one is classified as "being old." This is also the result of less people retiring from the workforce, with people who consider themselves young continuing to enjoy their work.

As the life cycles became more complex, the "average" lifestyle of the typical adult is disappearing. As people spend more years in learning institutions, and marriage and raising children become individual choices, the timing of these life stages varies by as much as 20 years between people. Career paths are changing and are not always uninterrupted. This is because of the rapidly changing social environment and long lifespans which have given people the option to quit their jobs, return to school, and start over in a new career. As a result, the lines that demarcated one's "social age" in which people used to ask themselves "What should I be doing at this age?" in terms of employment, parenthood, self-care, and retirement are blurring.

French sociologist Jean Viard describes the present times as an age of "interruption" in which society encourages people to constantly seek change rather than stay in one profession for too long. In an age where people have to change to stay competitive, people are not living in a linear sequence that goes from young age to middle-age to old but are living more in a series from Life #1 to Life #2, etc., giving people the chance to start over many times. This intermittent nature of modern life adds to uncertainty and anxiety over choosing a life path and at the same time blurs the line between identifying as an adult or a child.

As a result, the experiences of older generations can no longer serve as a reference for the next generation. The growing popularity of psychology and counseling content featuring mental health experts also reveals a cross-section of society today in which many adults have lost direction in life. For those who do not yet identify themselves as adults, support in the form of an "adult manual" is much needed.

It is also notable that parenting content is popular during times of low birth rates. However, the methods in which parenting advice is consumed is different from the past. Demand for such advice comes not only from parents with young children, but also from adults who want to understand their own childhood, or older parents who want to understand the present state of their grown children. Viewers are comforted by hearing that their problems are not their fault when they identify themselves with the content in the program. As mentioned in the "Generation Alpha" chapter, children are raised in a more affluent environment compared with the past, with ample pocket money. Paradoxically, this can be one of the factors that encourages immaturity.

Psychoanalysis shows that children need to experience loss in order to grow into an adult. Just as a baby experiences the weaning process, loss is a process of accepting that one cannot have everything one wants. When a child experiences loss and moves on to the next stage, the child learns how to move on to bigger goals. Yet those that grow up without lacking anything do not have the opportunity to experience loss, which is a crucial step in becoming an adult. This can leave people in a stage where their mental age and actual age do not match. This is due to the lack of social and psychological pressures that prepare them for adulthood.

In the past, children experienced loss naturally. The family rules, community norms, social ideology, and cultural traditions were mechanisms that played a role in making children independent. However, in the small family sizes of today, much of that has been replaced with individual choices, meaning less opportunity for young children to experience loss. Thus, people lose the motivation to change the course of their lives on their own – just like a child who does not want to leave their mother's arms.

Neverland's shadow

Professor Lee Young-Jun of Kyung Hee University points out in a column that when meeting an old friend at a 30-year reunion, westerners say *"Wow! You have changed so much!"* with the intention to say they have done well for themselves by improving so much. But at Korean reunions, it is a compliment to say *"Wow! You have not changed at all!"*

It is a compliment to say someone looks unchanged because that means they look young. But the flipside to this comment is that they are still immature. In that context, Neverland, filled with children, cannot just be a place that is filled with fun and positives. The negative aspects of a society obsessed with youth must be pointed out.

Although children are pure, they are also immature. Jean Piaget, who established a theory of cognitive development of children, classified the developmental process of children in four stages: sensorimotor stage, pre-operational stage, concrete operational stage, and formal operational stage. Within the stages are characteristics of children such as self-centeredness, believing inanimate objects are alive, following norms only to avoid punishment, focusing only on certain topics and ignoring others, to name a few. These characteristics of childhood can equally be applied to people with Neverland Syndrome: overly self-centered behavior, obsession with inanimate characters, blaming others or the government for their problems, and being too preoccupied with their own tastes.

Children are often caught up in their own worlds. Professor Tamami Katada, a Japanese psychiatrist, described this as "infantile omnipotence." It refers to the state of avoiding the gap between one's ideals and reality by believing that anything is possible. In this state, mental fortitude suffers and it becomes easy to fall into escapism and avoid responsibility. According to Katada, the social issues in Japan, such as social recluses and overbearing parents are, a symptom of lingering infantile omnipotence and a symptom of immaturity on a broader scale.

It's not just limited to Japan. In many developed countries including Korea, the number of people who have yet to find their life paths independent of their parents is increasing. People living with their parents and getting financial help are known as "parasite singles" in Japan and "KIPPERS (Kids in Parents' Pockets Eroding Retirement Savings)" in the UK. In Italy, they are called *"bamboccioni* (big babies)." As each term suggests, adult children who fail to achieve economic independence cause anxiety and erode the finances of their parents. In Korea, 64.1% of unmarried adult children aged 19 to 49 live with their parents, and when narrowed down to just forty-somethings, the proportion reaches 48.8%. Finding a solution is not easy given that it is not just the issue of the individual but a structural problem.

Outlook and Implications

By 2025, Korea is expected to be an aging society with more than 20% of the population over the age of 65. It is ironic that society is suffering from Neverland Syndrome amid the shift to an aging society. The Neverland society, which refuses to age, faces issues surrounding immaturity as we have mentioned, but it also offers a positive outlook. Even as people age, the market and society can retain vitality. A consumer market targeting Peter Pans also offers many advantages. In an anxiety-ridden society, childhood nostalgia offers psychological comfort, and focusing on having fun helps relieve the stress of adult life.

The refrain of a popular meme in the US is "adulting is hard." Young people who have never used a washing machine on their own or paid their bills are belatedly realizing the challenges of real life. To the older generations who were largely self-reliant and supported their family financially, this may seem immature. Yet, this thought that adults should be able to do certain tasks easily may also be a stereotype of the older generations.

The concept of "youth" was only coined after World War II, and "middle age" was also a concept that only arose in the latter half of the 20th century. What people assume as the typical appearance of middle-aged people is nothing more than the result of a stereotype that has existed for just one or two generations. Instead of being overly burdened by responsibilities, sharing memes such as "I don't want to be an adult today" and being open about the hardships of being an adult may be a new way to live as an adult.

"The tragedy of old age is not that one is old, but that one is young."

As Oscar Wilde put it, everyone thinks they are still young. If we don't consider ourselves old enough perhaps "adulthood" refers not to a specific point in our lives, but rather a process of development. The key point should not be "People are not very mature these days," but "How do we accumulate wisdom and experience without losing the curiosity of a child?" Life is a non-stop series of performances where people are required to immediately learn to perform when thrown on a stage, without any rehearsal. Like in Neverland, where people never stop learning, people today are just older children who are getting a little bit more mature, day by day.

2023
Consumer Trend Insights

초판 1쇄 발행 2022년 11월 30일

지은이 김난도, 전미영, 최지혜, 이수진, 권정윤,
        이준영, 이향은, 한다혜, 이혜원, 추예린, 전다현
번역 윤혜준
감수 미셸 램블린
펴낸이 성의현
펴낸곳 미래의창

등록 제10-1962호(2000년 5월 3일)
주소 서울시 마포구 잔다리로 62-1 미래의창빌딩(서교동 376-15, 5층)
전화 02-338-6064(편집), 02-338-5175(영업) **팩스** 02-338-5140
홈페이지 www.miraebook.co.kr
ISBN 978-89-5989-712-4 13320

※ 책값은 뒤표지에 있습니다.

생각이 글이 되고, 글이 책이 되는 놀라운 경험. 미래의창과 함께라면 가능합니다.
책을 통해 여러분의 생각과 아이디어를 더 많은 사람들과 공유하시기 바랍니다.
투고메일 togo@miraebook.co.kr (홈페이지와 블로그에서 양식을 다운로드하세요)
제휴 및 기타 문의 ask@miraebook.co.kr